A Thorogood Special Briefing

3rd Edition

EMPLOYMENT LAW ASPECTS OF MERGERS AND ACQUISITIONS – A PRACTICAL GUIDE

Michael Ryley

THOROGOOD

Thorogood Publishing Ltd
10-12 Rivington Street
London EC2A 3DU

t: 020 7749 4748
f: 020 7729 6110
e: info@thorogoodpublishing.co.uk
w: www.thorogoodpublishing.co.uk

A CIP catalogue record for this Special Briefing is available from the British Library.

ISBN 1 85418 726 0
978-185418 726-0

Printed in Great Britain
by Marston Digital

The author

Michael Ryley MA (Oxon), Solicitor, is a partner in the Employment Group at Pinsent Masons. He specialises in the commercial aspects of employment law and has a long-standing interest in the impact of business transfers on employees, a subject on which he has spoken and written extensively. He has considerable experience of acquisitions and disposals, both in the UK and abroad.

The author is a regular speaker/chairman at seminars on employment law topics and has written many articles on the subject, particularly on the impact of TUPE on business transfers. He is the author, with Professor Robert Upex, of *TUPE: Law and Practice* and, with Edward Goodwyn, of *Employment Law for the Construction Industry*.

Pinsent Masons is a full service commercial law firm with over 270 partners and more than 1,700 staff in the UK and internationally. The Employment Group is independently recognised as one of the best and most experienced teams of employment lawyers in the country.

Contents

Introduction

Introduction

The world of mergers and acquisitions will often appear intimidating to those who encounter it infrequently. A proliferation of jargon, bulky documentation and the sheer complexity of the issues conspire against a ready comprehension of the transaction.

One topic that almost invariably arises when companies and businesses are being bought and sold is employment law; the transaction will have to be effected with regard to its implications for the management of human resources. The fear of redundancies, concern over employee rights and the prospects for employees following the transfer are all issues of great concern for the employees of vendors and purchasers alike. Where the target of the proposed transaction is a major employer in the area, these concerns may become community-wide.

Sound HR management is essential to the welfare of any enterprise, engendering goodwill, enhancing the working environment and reducing the possibility of claims being brought against employers. It could be vital to the purchaser's prospects of unlocking the value in the company or business which is the target of the acquisition. Unless employee cooperation can be secured and motivation maintained, a smooth and successful transaction may be difficult to achieve.

The challenge, therefore, for the employment lawyer and for the HR manager is to achieve these HR management objectives within the context of the transaction, working as part of a larger team. The object of this report is to guide those involved with the employment law and HR issues, particularly the in-house lawyer and the HR manager, through those aspects of the transaction with which they need to be concerned. It seeks to identify the key practical and legal issues, to identify the documentation that needs to be drafted or reviewed by them and to set their role in the context of the transaction as a whole. The dominant perspective is that of the purchaser, given that it is the purchaser who tends to make the running and who is exposed to the greatest risk in a transaction of this nature.

This report seeks to identify the principal issues and explain common practice; it does not aspire to be a comprehensive treatise on the law in this area, which is increasingly complex, continually developing and full of pitfalls for the unwary. That is best left to other more detailed works. In outlining the relevant legal issues, however, the law is described as at 1st October 2010. Pensions law and practice, which might be expected to be of interest to lawyers and HR managers in the context of M&A transactions, is considered a subject in its own right outside the scope of this report and is dealt with only in passing.

This third edition has been revised with particular regard to the developments in the Courts and tribunals following the changes in the law introduced by the *Transfer of Undertakings (Protection of Employment) Regulations 2006* (S.I. 2006/246), which are abbreviated throughout to 'TUPE'. The *Council Directive on the approximation of the laws of the Member States relating to the safeguarding of employees' rights in the event of transfers of undertakings, businesses or parts of undertakings or businesses* (2001/23/EC), is referred to throughout as the Acquired Rights Directive.

Chapter 1
Overview: HR management issues and acquisition strategy

- What is 'M&A'?
- Employment law and HR management issues in context
- Putting the team together
- Documentation

Chapter 1
Overview: HR management issues and acquisition strategy

What is 'M&A'?

In referring to 'M&A', mergers and acquisitions, this report considers the employment law issues which arise on the transfer of a business or a body corporate from one owner to another. Examples of M&A transactions include:

- The acquisition of shares in a public listed company.
- A management buy-out.
- The sale of shares in a private company.
- A merger of two companies.
- Certain types of joint venture.
- The sale of a business, including the sale of a division of a company.
- An intra-group reorganisation.

In short, the subject matter of this report is the transfer of responsibility for the employees who work in an enterprise upon the transfer of ownership of that enterprise. All transactions must be considered in the light of their own particular facts, but it is nevertheless possible to address the subject of employee rights in M&A transactions in general terms, largely because all such transactions may be categorised either as share sales, where the ownership of the enterprise transfers by reason of the transfer of shares in a corporate entity, or as asset sales, where all or part of the economic components that make up the business of the enterprise are sold. This basic distinction is dealt with in more detail at page 28 below. The key to understanding the legal implications of M&A transactions is to classify each transaction into one category or the other.

Employment law and HR management issues in context

Although issues relating to employment law and HR management will arise in virtually all M&A transactions, their significance may be expected to vary considerably from transaction to transaction. Consider, for example the following three situations:

- A purchaser views the target business as being particularly attractive because of its market share. Following the acquisition, the purchaser proposes closing down certain manufacturing operations of the target and plans to integrate these within the purchaser's existing manufacturing resources. An important part of the post-acquisition strategy involves achieving economies of scale. Inevitably this will involve laying off a significant proportion of the target's workforce.

  In a transaction of this nature, the employees will be seen as a negative factor in the equation – the purchaser is concerned principally with assessing and minimising severance costs and associated liabilities. Employment issues will not be a high priority. The purchase price should be considered in the light of these latent liabilities.

- A purchaser is buying a target in which the employees are a major asset. The sales force has strong customer links and there are technical personnel who are the key to the target's competitive advantage in the market.

  In such circumstances employment issues may be the key to the purchaser unlocking the value in the target and employment issues will be seen in a positive light. Specific attention will be given to ensuring that employees transfer to the purchaser, that they are incentivised and that they are locked in to the target as far as possible. It may be that the purchaser will seek to link the payment of part of the consideration to the continued employment of key personnel and key man insurance may be put in place.

- There will not infrequently be a significant overlap between the workforce of the target and the community. The target may be a substantial employer in an area and therefore the prospects for the employees of the target following the acquisition may have a significant bearing on the prospects of the community generally. For example, wider community issues came to the fore in the acquisition by Nestlé of Rowntrees. The future of Rowntrees in York became a political issue;

employee relations issues widened to include public relations and political lobbying.

Attending to these employee/community relations issues can be the key to a successful acquisition. Such issues can be a determining factor in whether the transaction proceeds to completion.

It can be seen from these examples that employment issues will often vary considerably in significance. In any given case, there will probably be a mix of all three of the situations outlined above, to a greater or lesser extent. It is clear that the different circumstances outlined above are capable of giving rise to widely differing priorities and it is essential that in each proposed acquisition an understanding of the context of the employment law issues is achieved at an early stage. Not only does this aid in the approach to due diligence and the drafting of documentation, which may be more focused as a result, it allows employment law and HR management issues to take their proper place within the basket of factors that will need to be considered by the acquisition team when determining overall strategy and the structure of the transaction.

Putting the team together

M&A transactions are conducted by teams rather than by individuals. The size of the team that will be assembled to handle an acquisition or a disposal will vary from transaction to transaction. The team will consist of a mixture of management and advisors, both internal and external. It may include some or all of the following:

- Management – business development; treasury; incoming/outgoing management of the target itself; HR; etc.
- Lawyers – corporate; employment; real estate; pensions; etc.
- Accountants – due diligence; tax; etc.
- Investment bankers and corporate finance advisors.
- PR Consultants.

The larger the team, the greater the need for teamwork, good organisation and good communications within the team. For those responsible for employment law and HR management issues, it is important that they understand their position and role within the team and what is expected of them. It is important to get reporting lines and channels of communication, incoming and outgoing and within the team, firmly established at an early stage.

The following practical suggestions should be borne in mind by those responsible for employment law and HR management issues:

- Seek to become a member of the team as early as possible, in so far as that is practicable. Clearly, the sooner that employment lawyers and HR managers are brought on to the team, the earlier they will be able to contribute to overall strategic thinking. As is made clear in the previous section, it is important that the employment law and HR management issues are put into context at the outset. Typically, there will already be a team in place when employment lawyers and HR managers become involved. Early involvement of employment lawyers and HR managers, before the team is committed to a strategy, is essential if options are to be left open and HR issues are to be managed with flexibility.
- Ensure that clear lines of communication are established within the team. It is important that all members of the team are kept informed and that information received by one member of the team which is generally relevant is disseminated to other members of the team. The appropriate circulation lists need to be established and regular briefings issued. It may well be the case that information needs to be disseminated efficiently within the team whilst at the same time ensuring that the information does not leak beyond the team.
- Not only is effective information distribution important for management purposes, there may be legal implications if this is not achieved. If information has been received by one member of the team (for example, if information is given by the HR manager of the vendor to the HR manager of the purchaser), its receipt may be sufficient to establish deemed knowledge of that information on the part of the purchaser as a whole for certain legal purposes (such as to qualify the purchaser's liability under the warranties), notwithstanding that the member of the team in receipt of the information may have failed to disseminate the information to other members of the team. For that reason, it is particularly important that there is tight management of disclosure information – see chapter 2.
- Clear reporting lines should be established within the team at the outset.
- The generation of documents must be organised, with clear responsibility for drafting and reviewing each individual document. Those handling employment law and HR management issues will be responsible for the generation of certain documentation (such as correspondence with employee representatives); other documentation

will have an employment aspect but will be the responsibility of another member of the team (such as the sale and purchase agreement) and production of the document will require coordination and teamwork.

- Establishing direct contact with counterparts on the other side of the transaction is likely to be helpful. For example, the HR management team of the purchaser will have principal responsibility for HR issues – information on this topic could be collected most effectively from the HR managers of the target. However, this process cannot operate entirely independently; in particular, the disclosure of information by this process must be closely controlled.
- Clear lines of communication and demarcation of responsibility between internal personnel and external advisors should be established at the outset.

The efficient operation of the team is likely to be of considerable importance in the transaction as a whole. Those responsible for employment law and HR management must ensure that they participate fully in the working of the team.

Documentation

In order for those responsible for employment law and HR management issues to make an effective contribution, it is necessary that they have a general understanding of the documentation required in the transaction as a whole. This may be summarised in the following diagram:

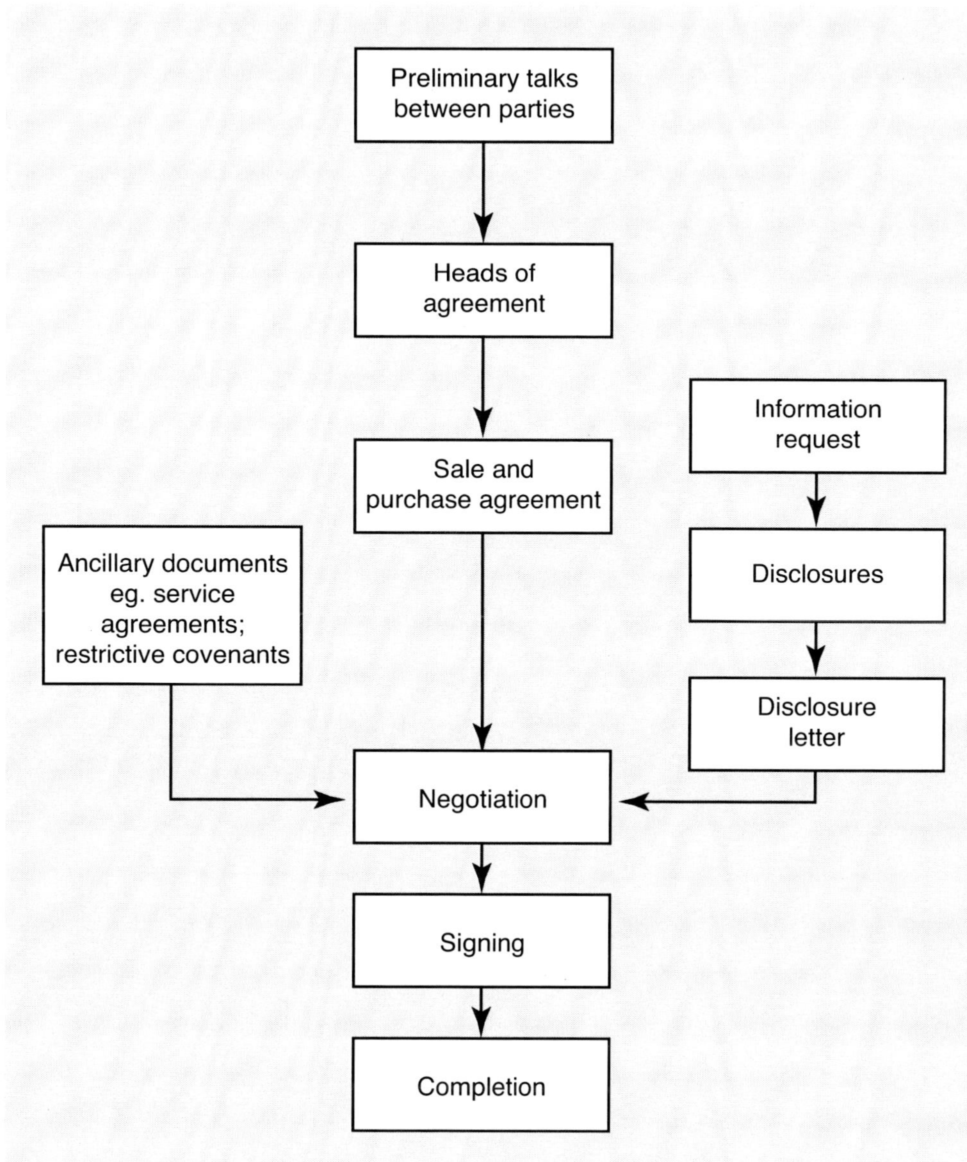

The document at the centre of the transaction is the **sale and purchase agreement**, which will govern all aspects of the transaction. A draft of this document may or may not be preceded by **heads of agreement**, an outline summary of the transaction that has been agreed, which are ordinarily drafted so that, for the most part, they are non-binding. A **disclosure letter** will be prepared in conjunction with the disclosure of documents by the vendor to the purchaser. In the sale and purchase agreement the purchaser will seek warranties regarding the nature and condition of the target. The disclosure of documents and other information contained in the disclosure letter will qualify the extent of those warranties.

In addition to these central documents, other documents of more specific relevance may need to be drafted; for example, new service agreements may be required for senior executives; restrictive covenants may need to be drafted; documents may need to be generated in order to disclose information to employee representatives; statements may be required to reflect changes to terms and conditions of employment.

Employment lawyers and HR managers will be concerned, therefore, with two distinct sets of documentation:

- It will be necessary to contribute to documents generated by others, such as those relating to the employment aspects of the sale and purchase agreement, in which there will be clauses specifically relating to employees and clauses of a general nature which will have an impact on employment issues.
- There will be documents to draft for which the employment lawyer and the HR manager will have principal responsibility, such as documents relating to the supply of information to employee representatives.

The documents which will be of relevance to those responsible for employment law and HR management issues are examined in detail in chapter 7.

It is important that employment law and HR management issues are addressed at the earliest opportunity. For example, a position may be taken on such important questions as whether TUPE will apply (for an overview of TUPE's implications see chapter 4) as early as the first draft of a set of heads of agreement. Employment law and HR management input must be considered at that stage; otherwise the scope for changing course at a later stage may already have been significantly limited.

Chapter 2
Understanding the target

- Generating information
- Due diligence: what to ask for; what to look for
- Data protection
- The vendor's perspective

Chapter 2
Understanding the target

Generating information

It is for the purchaser to ask such questions of the vendor as the purchaser thinks appropriate against a background of caveat emptor: buyer beware. It is common practice for the purchaser to satisfy himself as to the nature and condition of the target on the strength of information collected by the purchaser from a variety of sources, including that disclosed by the vendor, and on the basis of warranties and indemnities given by the vendor.

From the moment when the purchaser first forms an interest in the target, he is gradually building up a picture of the target. All the time he is seeking to form a view as to whether to make a purchase and, if so, on what terms. Shortly before the transaction is due to be effected, this process becomes more focused and the sale and purchase agreement will typically contain assurances concerning the key attributes of the target, in the form of warranties and indemnities. The warranties will be qualified and limited in extent by the information disclosed by the vendor.

A central objective of the members of the acquisition team during the course of the acquisition process will be the review of information. This is known as the process of due diligence. Information is essential in the context of a properly evaluated decision to purchase, specifically:

- Forming the decision as to whether to proceed with the purchase of the target.
- Enabling an accurate assessment to be made of the value of the target.
- Allowing the purchaser to begin to plan for the running of the target immediately following the acquisition.
- Allowing the purchaser to think ahead to various issues relating to the integration of the target into the purchaser's existing operations and in particular to the harmonisation of the terms and conditions of employment of the transferring employees with existing employees of the purchaser.

Those charged with responsibility for employment law and HR management issues will wish to analyse the human resources required by the target as early as possible. It is a fundamental part of putting employment law issues into context. An appreciation is needed of what resources are deployed in the target and this needs to be matched against the purchaser's business plans for the target post acquisition.

For the purposes of running financial models, information will be required about the payroll costs relating to the current workforce and other costs dependent upon the purchaser's plans, such as severance costs and costs relating to recruitment and relocation.

Both the purchaser and the vendor will have their own objectives in terms of the workforce. The best chance of achieving a swift agreement on employment law and HR management issues is where these strategies are complementary – for example, where the vendor is happy to see the workforce transfer to the purchaser and where the purchaser wishes to acquire the workforce. In cases where there is a disparity of objectives, the position becomes more difficult. This often generates arguments as to whether or not the purchaser is prepared to accept responsibility for all or part of the workforce and whether the price should be adjusted to take account of severance liabilities, for example where the purchaser perceives that the target is overstaffed; there may also be something of a scramble as to which employees are transferred to the purchaser and which remain with the vendor.

Once the purchaser has developed an outline strategy in the context of existing and anticipated resources, employment law and HR management issues can then be put into context within the bigger picture. An acquisition strategy is likely to be developed with regard to a wide range of factors including employment law, tax, real estate and contractual issues.

Not only must information be gathered, its reliability must be investigated and, wherever possible, assured through verification and warranties. Sources of information may be expected to include the following:

- **Information requests**: these take the form of a 'shopping list', ordinarily prepared by the purchaser's solicitors and delivered to the vendor's solicitors. It is an opportunity to ask for whatever information the purchaser considers appropriate to his evaluation of the target. Clearly, although there may be an element of 'boilerplate' to such requests, whereby items of invariable relevance are requested, the efficacy of the request is likely to be related directly to the extent to which the request is tailored to the particular circumstances of each individual case.

A sample information request is set out in chapter 7 of this report at page 78, accompanied by drafting notes.

- **Information in the public domain**: a substantial body of information may be available in the public domain, and this may be particularly valuable in the context of a hostile acquisition, where the cooperation of the target may not be available or where the prospect of an acquisition remains confidential. HR information is likely to be available from sources such as the annual report and accounts of the target; from media searches (particularly in relation to industrial relations, pay settlements and employee claims); from inside sources such as existing employees, and from analysts.
- **Accountant's report**: accountancy due diligence may be expected to generate information relating to HR issues, particularly in relation to payroll costs and administration.
- **Site visits**: if and when allowed on to the site or given access to HR management, a good deal of information may be generated. Questions can be asked and the disclosure of information in a discussion format may be particularly useful to the purchaser. The vendor should commit such orally disclosed information to paper in order that it may form part of the bundle of disclosed information and hence operate to qualify the warranties in the sale and purchase agreement.
- **TUPE information**: Regulation 11 of TUPE requires the transferor to notify to the transferee the following employee liability information in respect of everyone assigned to the transferring undertaking:
  - the identity and age of the employee
  - a statement of terms and conditions (covering those items which an employer is required to put in writing under section 1 of the Employment Rights Act 1996)
  - information regarding disciplinary and grievance proceedings involving any transferring employee (any disciplinary procedure taken against an employee, or any grievance procedure taken by an employee, within the previous two years in circumstances where a Code of Practice issued under Part IV of the Trade Union and Labour Relations (Consolidation) Act 1992, which relates exclusively or primarily to the resolution of disputes applies (that

is to say, for practical purposes, where the ACAS Code of Practice on Disciplinary and Grievance Procedures applies)

– information regarding any court or tribunal claim brought by an employee against the transferor within the last two years, or that the transferee has reasonable grounds to believe that an employee may bring

– details of any collective agreement that will have effect after the transfer.

This information needs to be accurate as at a date within 14 days of the date when given and must be given not later than 14 days before the transfer, being updated if there is any change. Failure to comply exposes the transferor to the risk of a claim for compensation, which should not ordinarily be less than £500 per employee.

- **Disclosure letter**: as the sale and purchase agreement is drafted, the vendor will wish to disclose information to restrict his liability under the warranties which the purchaser is seeking. This takes two forms: information recorded in the body of the disclosure letter and documents annexed in the disclosure bundle.

The generation of information which will be disclosed against the warranties may be summarised by reference to the following simplified model:

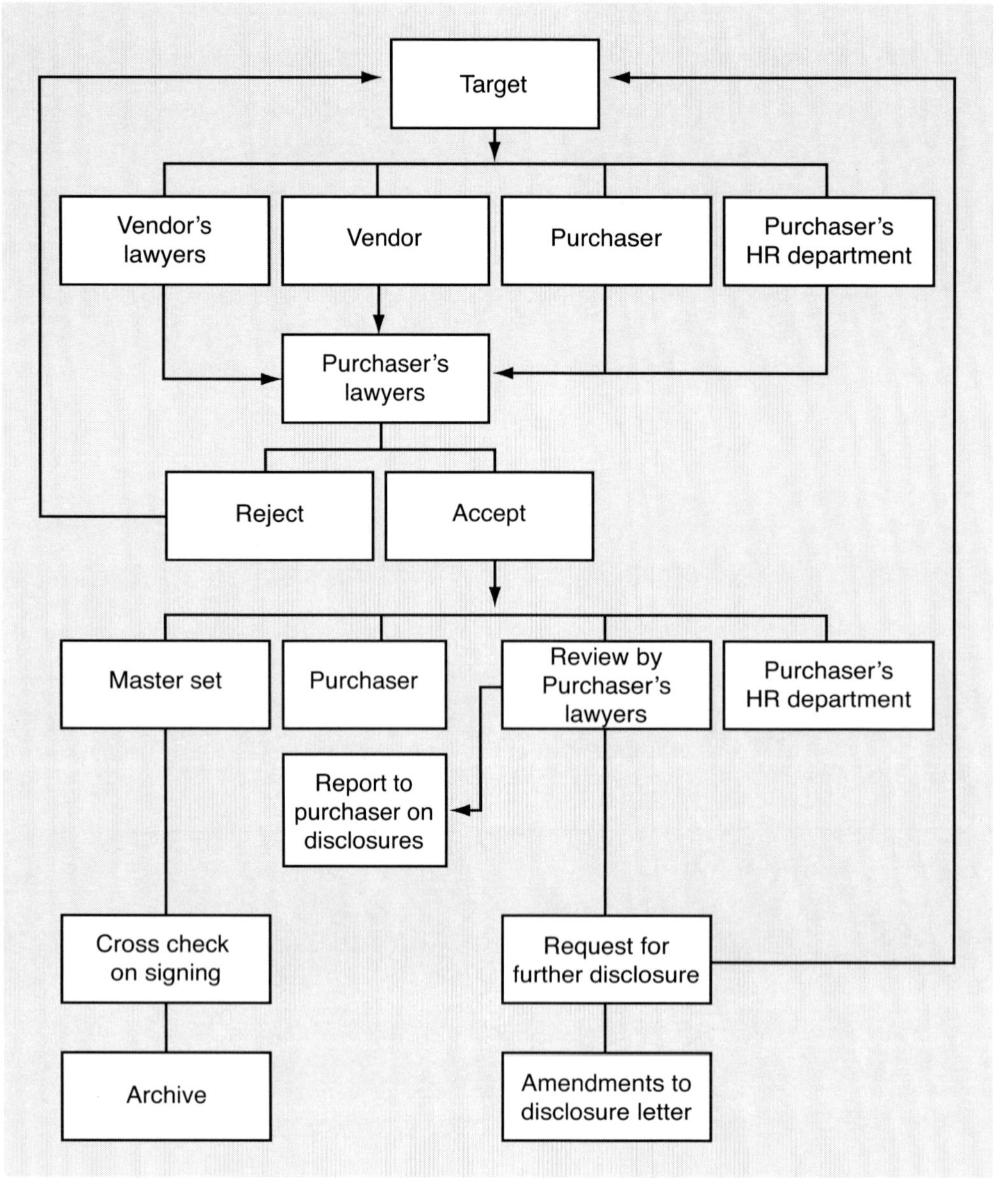

1. Information is produced concerning the target. It may come to the attention of the purchaser via a number of different routes – for example, information may be supplied by the target to its lawyers and then passed on to the purchaser's lawyers. Equally, it may be disclosed directly to the purchaser, for example in the course of discussions between the target's HR managers and the purchaser's HR managers. However it is disclosed, it is particularly important that an accurate record is kept by both vendor and purchaser of what has been disclosed. In particular, the vendor's solicitor must ensure that everything disclosed is recorded as being disclosed and cross indexed to the disclosure letter.

Otherwise, it will be difficult for the vendor to claim at a later stage that the purchaser was aware of the content of that information. A properly drafted sale and purchase agreement will ensure that only the information which is ultimately contained in the disclosure bundle, which will be cross-indexed to the disclosure letter or is within the text of the disclosure letter itself, is deemed to be within the knowledge of the purchaser (although the extent to which the purchaser may rely on such a clause was cast into doubt in *Eurocopy plc v Teesdale* [1992] BCLC 1067).

It must be made clear to all the members of the purchaser's acquisition team that all information must be passed on to the purchaser's solicitors to be recorded and reviewed.

2. Once that information has been received, it may be appropriate simply to reject it. For example, computer printouts of HR information may be generated without an index to explain the nature of the information. Whilst intelligible to the target, they may be of little or no value to the purchaser. Alternatively, the information may simply be illegible or incomplete. A request may be made to supply the information in complete and intelligible form.

3. Information may be acceptable but may be incomplete or may raise further questions which should be dealt with by way of supplemental enquiries. The purchaser should never be afraid to raise enquiries and is entitled to expect a proper answer.

4. If information is accepted by the purchaser then it should be copied and dealt with in a number of ways:

    - A master set of all information disclosed should be retained. This will form the basis of the disclosure bundle and will be an accurate record of information that has been accepted for disclosure purposes. The content of that bundle will need to be cross-checked by the vendor's lawyers and the purchaser's lawyers at the time at which the warranties are entered into.

    - A set of documents should be copied to the purchaser in order that it may be distributed internally to all those affected and may subsequently be analysed. For example, HR information should be fed through to the purchaser's HR department for their information and for their review.

- A review of the information disclosed should be carried out by the purchaser's solicitor. In the case of information relating to HR matters, this would ordinarily be done by the employment lawyer within the team. This will allow specialist consideration of the current circumstances of HR management within the target, as well as comment on the information's implications for the future HR management of the target by the purchaser, which may prompt a request for further disclosure.
- The information may lead to further enquiries, further consideration of the acquisition by the purchaser and a possible revision of the purchase price. The disclosure letter will continue to be updated and negotiated against this background.

Due diligence: what to ask for; what to look for

Although it is important that information is accumulated in order that the purchaser may begin to plan for the post-acquisition phase, the principal objectives of the due diligence exercise will be:

- To evaluate the target.
- To discover and quantify any hidden liabilities.

In the context of HR information, the following information is likely to be particularly significant and should be considered in the initial phase of due diligence:

- Payroll information – what is the cost of employing the workforce in the target? How does this compare with expectations and industry norms? What is the additional cost of engaging other workers such as consultants and sub-contractors?
- How adequate is the workforce for the needs of the target? How suited is it to the achievement of the purchaser's objectives?
- What additional training/redeployment/relocation costs may be expected to arise in the light of the purchaser's proposals?
- Are there accumulated liabilities such as extensive accrued holiday entitlements, particularly where there is an entitlement to receive cash in lieu?
- On what basis are non-employee workers engaged? How crucial are they to the business? Can arrangements be put in place to secure their continued participation in the business?

- What is the likely cost of any redundancies that may be required? Information needs to be put together to calculate the statutory entitlement, notice pay liability and any entitlements under a contractual enhanced redundancy payment scheme.
- Is there anything about the pay structure or the profile of the workforce which gives rise to a concern about possible discrimination? When was a job evaluation and pay structure review last carried out?
- Which employees is the vendor intending to withhold from the transfer? Are any key workers not transferring? Have workers been brought into the target recently with a view to transferring them to the purchaser?
- What restrictive covenants and incentives are in place to retain employees or at least to limit the consequences of their leaving? Key employees should be identified with a view to their retention being linked to completion of the transaction or to payment of the full purchase price.
- Is there anything particularly noticeable about the workforce? Is it comprised of particularly long serving workers or is there a very high turnover of staff? How does that compare with the purchaser's expectations? Is the age profile unusually old or young?
- Are there any unusual terms and conditions in the staff handbook and other terms and conditions of employment applicable to employees?
- Are the senior executives' service contracts reasonable or is their remuneration excessive?
- What sickness and disability benefits are in place? To what extent are these covered by insurance? What is the cost of the premiums?
- Details of all staff benefits – the cost of these will need to be reviewed and a view taken as to whether they are excessively generous.
- Details of union membership (as far as can be ascertained). Which unions are recognised? What collective agreements are in place?
- Are there any consultative bodies in place such as staff councils, works councils etc.?
- What is the recent industrial relations history of the target?
- Are there any claims outstanding made by employees against the target? What is the recent claims history like – both in relation to employment rights and industrial injuries?

- What is the accident book like? Have there been any recent visits from the Health and Safety Executive? What recommendations have been made by them?
- What equal opportunities policies and initiatives are there in place? Have there been any Equality and Human Rights Commission (or its predecessors) investigations? If so, what conclusions were reached?
- The whole question of pensions will need to be addressed, with particular regard to what rights and liabilities transfer, although this is a detailed issue which is outside the scope of this report.

Data protection

It is likely that personnel information required by the purchaser in connection with due diligence, and subsequently for HR management purposes following the transfer, will be held by the target in machine readable form, most likely on computer. The *Data Protection Act 1998* applies to such data and there are implications for all parties. Even where personnel information is held in manual files the Act will apply if the files fall into the definition of a 'relevant filing system'. This means, put broadly, that the file is highly structured and specific information about employees can be found easily in the file.

The information may be held by the target or by a third party, such as another group company or a computer bureau, on behalf of the target. In the course of the transaction such information will be transferred to professional advisors, such as solicitors, and to the purchaser itself. To the extent that any of those parties will be a transferor or a transferee of information, it is essential that the provisions of the *Data Protection Act 1998* are adhered to.

It is a criminal offence to hold data without having made a notification. A register of notifications is maintained by the Information Commissioner and the register contains details of data that is held, the purposes for which the data is held, and also describes the classes of transferee to whom the data may be disclosed. Therefore, any party which proposes to disclose data must check that it is registered with the Information Commissioner and that the notification covers the proposed transfer. The transferee must ensure that it is registered in respect of the information to be received, in relation to the purposes for which the information is to be held and used.

Any party transferring information must ensure that the register entry covers the purpose of disclosing information to a prospective purchaser in the context of a possible change of ownership of the target.

In the event that a party has not notified appropriately it will be necessary either to lodge an application for registration or to amend the registration. The notification can be carried out via the website at www.ico.gov.uk or by telephone (telephone 0303 123 1113). Alternatively, it may be appropriate simply to amend an existing registration.

The vendor must ensure that he is compliant with the Act when disclosing personal data. Identifying information should not be disclosed unless it is necessary for the purposes of the sale. Where disclosure is necessary, sensitive personal data (such as information on sickness records, convictions and political leanings) should not be included in the disclosures. The general rule is that individuals should be informed how their personal data is to be used and disclosed, to ensure that they are treated fairly. Clearly, there may be difficulties in telling employees of a proposed sale of a business: however the Act does not include any specific exemptions for these circumstances. The best option for the vendor therefore is to only disclose anonymised data as far as possible and, if other data has to be disclosed, ensure that it does not include sensitive data and surround it with confidentiality and security safeguards as described below.

Further guidance on this topic may be found on the Information Commissioner's Office website at www.ico.gov.uk and the reader's attention is drawn in particular to the Data Protection Good Practice Note, Disclosure of employee information under TUPE.

The vendor's perspective

The vendor will be principally concerned with receiving the largest possible purchase price with as little exposure to recourse by the purchaser as possible. The vendor's perspective is therefore rather different from that of the purchaser, who is engaged in an exercise of investigation and evaluation. The following are particular issues which the vendor should have in mind at an early stage in the transaction:

- Information should never be disclosed by the vendor until a binding confidentiality agreement has been entered into by the transferee. This agreement should provide that the information:
  - may not be transferred to a third party
  - will be returned if the transaction does not proceed to completion, together with all copies
  - may only be used for certain specified purposes related to the proposed transaction.
- At an initial stage, part of the information requested may be so sensitive that it is inappropriate to disclose it until the eleventh hour, in that its disclosure in circumstances where the transaction does not proceed to completion may be detrimental to the target's continuing business. In these circumstances consider:
  - a phased disclosure of information starting with the least sensitive information
  - disclosing information with certain items blanked out/omitted, to be disclosed at a later stage
  - the use of a data room, whereby information is made available to the purchaser and to the purchaser's representatives, but with a prohibition on taking copies.
- It is in the interests of the vendor that the scope for the purchaser to seek redress under the warranties in the sale and purchase agreement is kept to a minimum. In this respect, widespread and comprehensive disclosure of information is to be recommended. To the extent that the warranties are qualified, the purchaser is precluded from bringing a claim under the warranties in respect of the shortcomings of the target of which the purchaser was aware prior to the transfer.

- A careful record should be kept of all information disclosed. This should ultimately be contained in the disclosure letter or in the bundle of documents attached to the disclosure letter to ensure that the information has the effect of qualifying the warranties.

- Information delivered orally should be recorded either in the body of the disclosure letter itself or by a written memorandum which is then included within the bundle of documents annexed to the disclosure letter.

- If certain key employees are to be retained by the vendor, they should be transferred out of the target prior to completion. It is not unheard of for the vendor to move employees into the target shortly before completion of the transaction so as to transfer them out of the vendor's employment.

- It should be noted that the benefit of employment contracts will be lost as well as the burden where employees transfer under TUPE or where shares are sold. Particular attention should be given to restrictive covenants. If, for example, in a share sale there is an employee who has in his employment contract a restrictive covenant that relates not only to the target but to other group companies, a separate restrictive covenant should be entered into prior to completion in favour of the remaining group companies. Where TUPE applies, fresh restrictive covenants should be entered into to achieve a similar effect. This is a difficult area and specialist advice is likely to be needed.

- The vendor may well be sensitive to industrial relations issues surrounding the proposed transaction. Consideration should be given to restricting the purchaser's ability to make announcements and the content of those announcements.

A Thorogood Special Briefing

Chapter 3
Choosing an acquisition structure – implications for employees

- The share sale/asset sale distinction
- Employment law issues in share sales
- Employment law issues in non-TUPE asset sales
- TUPE: rationale
- Determining whether TUPE applies
- Insolvencies

Chapter 3
Choosing an acquisition structure – implications for employees

The share sale/asset sale distinction

Acquisitions and disposals invariably fit into two categories:

- Transfers of companies by the sale of shares.
- Transfers of businesses by the sale of assets.

This distinction is central to the way in which the transaction will be structured and documented, affecting a wide range of commercial issues. It is particularly significant in the context of employment issues.

In buying shares, the purchaser takes the company en bloc, with all its tax history, trading relationships, assets and liabilities. The purchaser is put in the position of assuming control of the company as a going concern by a straightforward and simple method, namely the mere transfer of shares. The sale of shares stands apart from the target itself, it being a transaction between the shareholder(s) of the company and the purchaser/prospective shareholder.

In buying assets, by contrast, the purchaser chooses what he wishes to buy from amongst the assets of the target business. Each asset needs to be acquired individually – land has to be conveyed, individual contracts novated and so forth. Liabilities may be left behind; those assets which are not required need not be purchased. The purchaser may concentrate his attention on those parts of the business which will deliver value post-acquisition. This route is likely to be particularly attractive where the vendor is insolvent, where there is doubt as to hidden liabilities, or where the purchaser is buying only a part of the operations of an enterprise.

The decision as to which structure to adopt will be taken on the basis of a number of factors, of which employment law issues are only one. That distinction, however, is likely to be central to the employment law implications of the transaction and should be borne in mind at all times. In fact, the distinction is refined slightly in terms of the employment law implications of the choice of structure, where it may be summarised as follows:

- Share sales.
- Asset sales – where TUPE does not apply.
- Asset sales – where TUPE does apply.

These three categories are considered in turn in the following sections of this report.

Employment law issues in share sales

The transfer of the shares in a company from vendor to purchaser leaves the employment relationship intact and unaffected by the transfer. The employment relationship is essentially a contractual one between the company and the employee and, by buying shares, a purchaser acquires the established contractual relationships between the target company and its employees; the status quo ante is maintained.

The principal employment law feature of a share sale for prospective purchasers is that TUPE has no application – hence issues of HR management may be handled free from the considerations which arise in an asset sale to which TUPE applies, which can prove particularly restrictive. This may be particularly important in relation to issues such as dismissals and the harmonisation of terms and conditions of employment.

The following are the principal practical employment law/HR management issues to consider in share sales:

- In a share sale, the purchaser acquires assets and liabilities regardless of whether he is aware of them. Due diligence is particularly important for the purchaser, in order that the purchase may be made with the purchaser's eyes opened. The purchaser will wish to inform himself about the nature of the workforce, the basis on which it is employed and any attendant liabilities. This should be reinforced by warranties in the share purchase agreement.
- Care should be taken to note that, even though the legal consequences of the share transfer may be limited, the employees' perception may be one of considerable change, particularly where there are significant changes in senior management and changes of policy between

incoming and outgoing shareholders. This should be addressed as an important employee relations issue. Save where works councils are in place or under the provisions of the Takeover Code, there are no legal obligations to disclose information to employee representatives and to consult with them analogous to those which arise in relation to asset sales governed by TUPE, but consultation and the disclosure of information undertaken voluntarily may have the effect of allaying concern.

- Are there members of the workforce who are not employees of the target company, for example consultants or employees of another group company providing services to the target? In such circumstances it may be necessary to enter into new contracts with the suppliers of such labour, if these workers are needed on a continuing basis.
- If key workers in the target company are employed by a third party and the purchaser wishes to recruit them as employees of the company, they cannot be transferred to the purchaser by agreement between the purchaser and the current employer without the agreement of the employee concerned: see *Nokes v Doncaster Amalgamated Collieries* [1940] AC 1014. Hence it would be necessary to secure the release of the employee from his current employer and to enter into a contract of employment between the employee and the target company to commence on the acquisition. In appropriate circumstances, it may be that a secondment agreement could be entered into whereby the vendor remains as the employer but the employees remain in the target to work at the direction of the purchaser.
- Notwithstanding that the contract of employment remains intact, there may be changes forced on the company by reason of moving out of a group of companies. For example, it may not be possible for the employees of the target company to continue to participate in the vendor's group pension scheme. In such circumstances, a scheme providing similar benefits would have to be established to avoid liability for breach of contract. Other employee benefits such as bonus schemes and incentive schemes may likewise have to be changed. Restrictive covenants may require reconsideration in the light of circumstances post-acquisition.

Employment law issues in non-TUPE asset sales

In an asset sale, the purchaser may pick and choose which assets he buys and which liabilities he is prepared to take on, in contrast to a share sale where there is an acquisition of the target en bloc. Employees, however, are an important exception to this general rule.

Where TUPE applies to the sale of assets (and the question of when TUPE applies is dealt with below), there is an automatic transfer of employees from vendor to purchaser by operation of law. The purchaser has no choice as to whether he takes on the employees engaged in the business or as to the terms upon which he engages them.

Where TUPE does not apply to the sale of assets, the purchaser takes the assets and the employees remain as employees of the vendor. The purchaser has no choice. As mentioned in the previous section, the purchaser and the vendor are not at liberty to agree amongst themselves that all or any employees will transfer from the employment of the vendor to the employment of the purchaser. Having said that, the purchaser will be at liberty to offer employment to some or all of the employees working pre-transfer in the target business, and the purchaser has complete discretion over the terms of any such offer.

The significance of the fact that there is no transfer of employees by operation of law will depend on the importance of the employees to the purchaser, for the purchaser cannot pick and choose amongst the workforce as he may otherwise wish to pick and choose amongst the assets of the vendor business. For there to be a transfer of employees, this would have to be done with the consent of the employees themselves and with the consent of their current employer to release them.

Where the workforce has no particular value to the purchaser, such as where there are no specialised skills or customer contacts within the sales force, the purchaser has a choice:

- Either he can offer employment to all or some of the employees on whatever terms he chooses, without the employees retaining continuity of employment; or
- He may refuse to offer employment without fear of liability; the vendor will be left with any redundancy costs.

Where the workforce or a part of the workforce is essential to the purchaser's business plan post-acquisition, the purchaser must seek:

- To restructure the transaction to ensure that TUPE applies; or
- To recruit from the workforce, conditional on the transfer proceeding to completion.

The cooperation of the vendor is likely to be required, given that the employees will be under contract. The purchaser may wish to make the purchase subject to satisfactory completion of this recruitment exercise. In practice, if the employees are facing redundancy from the vendor, they are likely to accept an offer of employment from the purchaser.

TUPE: rationale

TUPE supersedes the *Transfer of Undertakings (Protection of Employment) Regulations 1981*, which were introduced with marked reluctance by the UK Government in order to implement the Acquired Rights Directive. By reason of TUPE's principal purpose, to implement the Directive into UK law, TUPE is invariably interpreted in the light of the Directive and of European case law.

The Directive's origins may be traced to the laws of those member states which have similar provisions. France, for example, has had such laws in place since the 1920s. It was felt that it made sense that, where assets are transferred, the people with the skills to realise the value of those assets should be transferred also. This could be argued as having a macro-economic benefit for the French economy as a whole and at the same time protecting employee rights and promoting stability of employment.

The UK had no such law prior to the introduction of TUPE and the introduction of TUPE was a novel concept, the principal implication being that a transfer of a business may result in the transfer of those employees engaged in the business, together with all rights and liabilities including continuity of employment, as if they had always been employees of the purchaser of the business. This had an immediate impact on the practice of purchasers in asset sales recruiting the redundant employees of the vendor on inferior terms and conditions of employment and without continuity of employment being preserved.

TUPE's central features may be summarised as:

- Increasing job security for employees on the transfer of a business through the preservation of contractual and statutory rights.
- Protection in the case of dismissal: not only will employees not suffer a break in continuity of employment (with potential consequences for their right to claim that they have been unfairly dismissed) but there is a rebuttable presumption that any dismissal connected with the transfer will be automatically unfair.
- A duty on employers to inform and, in certain circumstances, to consult with employee representatives.
- A transfer of collective rights.

Determining whether TUPE applies

Although the question of whether TUPE applies is a crucial one in terms of the employment law consequences of a transaction, it is remarkably difficult to arrive at the answer, such is the state of uncertainty in this area of the law. The practical advice is, therefore, that a considered view should always be formed as to whether TUPE applies, but the sale/purchase agreement should be drafted in such a way that it deals with what happens if this working assumption is subsequently found to have been incorrect. Through warranties and indemnities it should be possible to 'hedge' against a contrary interpretation on this point by a court or tribunal, provided always that it is practicable to negotiate a contract in these terms and that the other party to the contract has the means to meet any claim under the warranties and indemnities in the contract.

Is this an asset sale?

As explained above, TUPE has no application to share sales.

Is the subject of the transaction an 'undertaking'?

TUPE applies on the transfer of an undertaking, business or a part of an undertaking or business. Regrettably, the term 'undertaking' is left undefined, although the term 'business' is less open to doubt. It matters not whether the target is run for profit-making purposes.

TUPE applies as much to the transfer of a part of an undertaking or business as to the transfer of the entire undertaking or business. Hence it could apply, for example, to the sale of a division of a company or to the sale of the part of a business carried on at a particular location, such as the sale of one of two manufacturing sites.

The concept of an undertaking is clearly wider than the mere transfer of a business in the conventional sense. The overwhelming majority of asset sales in the M&A context will be governed by TUPE, particularly where the purchaser has a clear intention to acquire a business as a going concern and the transaction will therefore result in the transfer of a substantial proportion of the key assets of the business. The difficult area is where only a limited collection of assets are to be acquired. The issue might be illustrated as follows. Assume that a piece of equipment is capable of manufacturing a product. The mere acquisition of a piece of equipment is not a transfer of an undertaking or business. However, the piece of equipment interacts with a number of other assets to create a business: for example, the right to occupy the place where it is situated; materials; the person who operates the machine; contracts for the sale of the products made on the machine, to name but a few. How many of these assets need to be acquired before the sum total of assets acquired amounts to the transfer of a business or undertaking? It can sometimes be difficult to determine when this boundary has been crossed.

In *Schmidt v Spar-und Leihkasse der früheren Ämter Bordesholm, Kiel und Cronshagen* [1994] IRLR 302, the Advocate General of the European Court held that the following factors could be identified as underlying the concept of an undertaking:

- An economic unit or a business referable to a unit.
- A minimum level of organisational independence.
- Capable of existing by itself or as part of a larger unit.

In many M&A cases, the answer to whether or not there is an undertaking will be readily apparent. Where the answer is not clear cut, however, the issue should be approached with caution and specialist advice taken.

Having identified that the subject of the transaction amounts to an undertaking, the next question to ask is whether there is a transfer. There are two key issues:

- Does the undertaking retain its identity upon the transfer?
- Is there a change in the employer?

The most helpful decision of the European Court of Justice in this respect is in *Spijkers v Gebroeders Benedik Abbatoir* [1986] ECR 1119. The Court described the test as whether 'the business in question retains its identity in as much as it is transferred as a going concern, which may be indicated in particular by the fact that its operation is actually continued or resumed by the new employer with the same or similar activities.'

The Court laid out some examples of criteria which should be considered as part of a general review of all the facts of the case, no one criteria being conclusive of itself:

- The type of undertaking.
- Whether tangible assets (buildings, moveable property, etc.) are transferred.
- Whether intangible assets are transferred and the extent of their value.
- Whether the majority of the employees are taken on by the new employer.
- Whether customers are transferred.
- The degree of similarity between the activities carried on before and after the transfer.
- The period for which the activities were suspended (if any).

At some point, which will vary from case to case, a sufficient number of items from this list will transfer so that the point is reached where the undertaking itself can be said to have transferred. The purpose of the parties is likely to have a material bearing on the analysis of the tribunal. The importance of goodwill has been over emphasised, but it will be appreciated that this is often the breath that transforms the dry bones of a collection of assets into a living business.

Again, in many M&A transactions it will be clear that there is a transfer of an undertaking, particularly where the overt purpose of the purchaser is to acquire a business with a view to continuing to operate that business in its current form post-acquisition. The definitions within TUPE will, however, inevitably create problem cases. Where the answer to the question of whether there is a transfer is not clear, specialist advice will be required.

In *Rygaard v Stro Molle Akustik* [1996] IRLR 51, the European Court held that for an entity to transfer under TUPE it must be 'stable'. Hence the transfer of a business with a limited life could not constitute a transfer of an undertaking. In that case, the undertaking concerned involved the completion of joinery work on a building. Come the end of the building project, the undertaking would cease to have effect.

The practical difficulties that can occur in distinguishing between the mere sale of assets and the transfer of an undertaking may be illustrated by the case of *Woodhouse v Peter Brotherhood* [1972] 2 QB 520. In that case, a factory used in a diesel engine manufacturing business was sold and subsequently used in a business manufacturing turbines and spinning machines. Equipment was transferred and employees commenced employment with the purchaser. The Court held, however, that there was not a transfer of an undertaking. All that had happened was that there had been a transfer of assets and the subsequent commencement of a business similar to (but not the same as) the business prior to the sale.

Another example of different activities before and after the sale giving rise to the conclusion that there had been a mere transfer of assets and therefore there had not been a transfer of an undertaking can be seen in the Employment Appeal Tribunal's decision in *Mathieson v United News Shops* (EAT 554/94). In that case, a shop run in a portakabin at a hospital selling sweets, newspapers and the like and run by the hospital administration was replaced in a redevelopment of the hospital foyer area by a branch of a major chain convenience store selling an expanded range of items including toys, clothes and CDs. The fact that there was no transfer of premises, different product ranges, different hours of opening and a different trading philosophy led to the conclusion that there was no transfer of an undertaking.

Borderline cases are always going to cause problems, not least because it may be some while before the issue is brought before an employment tribunal, if at all. Therefore, the practical answer is to attempt to reach agreement between the parties as to whether the transaction is covered by TUPE. If there is agreement on whether TUPE applies and if the possibility of a tribunal decision reaching a contrary conclusion is covered by the terms of the sale/purchase agreement so as to restore the balance originally envisaged by the parties, the parties may go forward into the transaction with a degree of confidence.

Is the target situated in the UK?

Regulation 3(1)(a) of TUPE provides that, for TUPE to apply, the undertaking or part being transferred must be situated in the UK immediately before transfer. Hence the location of the parties and the law governing the transaction are of no consequence. For example, where a deal is struck between two American companies to sell a worldwide business governed by a sale/purchase agreement drawn up under the law of a state within the United States and where there is a transfer of a business in the UK, TUPE is capable of applying to the transaction to the extent that it relates to the UK business.

TUPE can also apply to overseas employees of the business. For example, on the sale of a UK-based business selling its products worldwide, a Far East sales manager, based overseas, would transfer to the purchaser under TUPE even if his contract of employment was governed by a law other than English law, assuming that such employee was participating in the UK business as opposed to a discrete overseas business.

What happens if the transaction does not complete?

The fact that discussions are underway concerning an acquisition or a disposal will ordinarily have no effect on the employment status of the employees engaged in the target. TUPE applies with effect from completion of the transaction to transfer employees from vendor to purchaser.

There will occasionally be circumstances, however, where the purchaser assumes control of the target in advance of formal completion. For example, if the target business was in financial difficulties, the purchaser may be allowed to take control of the running of the business in advance of completion. In such circumstances, if the employees in the target begin to work under the control of the purchaser, the business having in effect been transferred to the purchaser, TUPE would apply at that stage. If there is subsequently a failure to complete the transaction and the business reverts to the vendor, TUPE would apply to transfer the employees back to the vendor.

Determining whether TUPE applies – the key questions

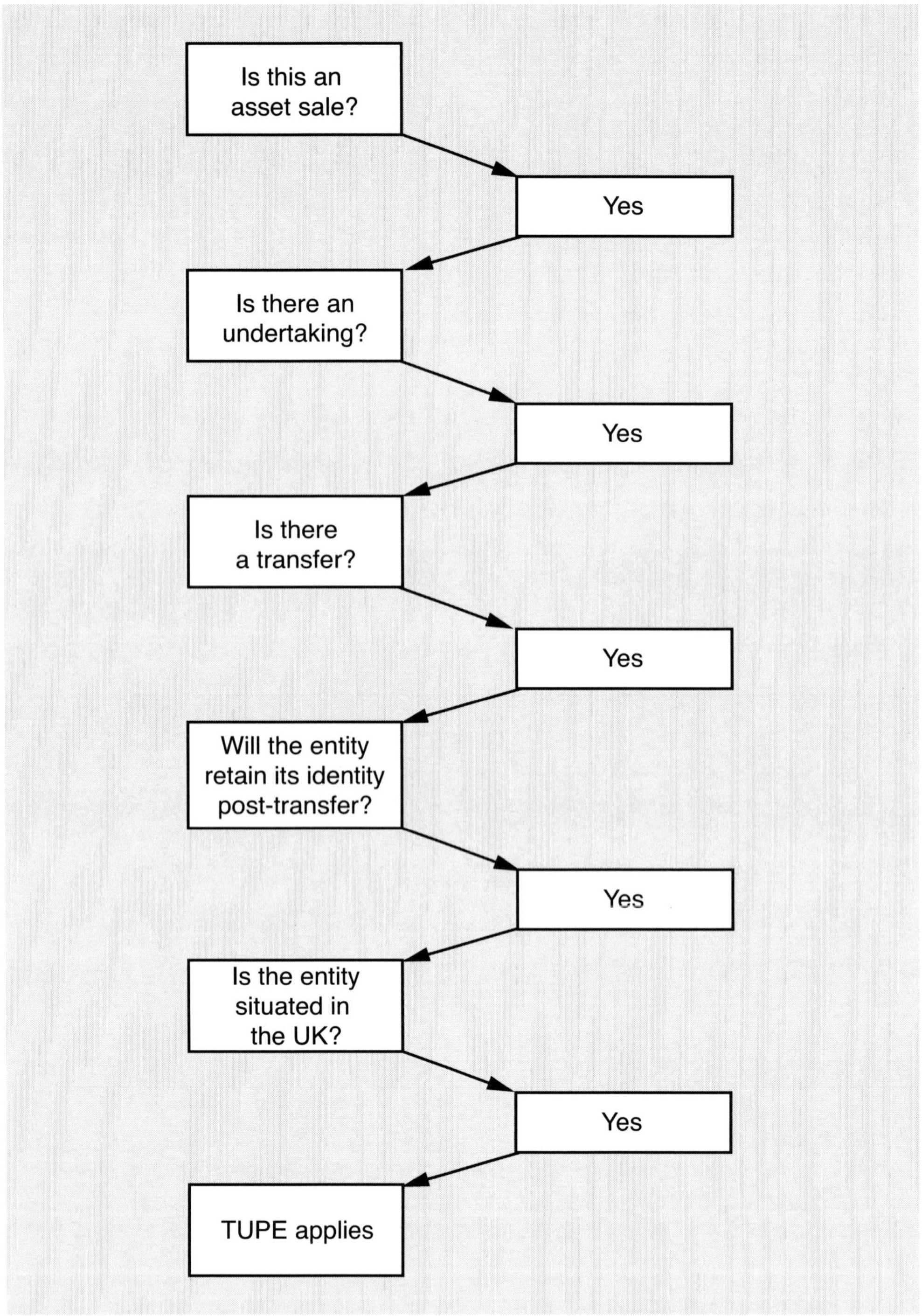

Insolvencies

Great care should be taken when buying a business from a receiver or administrator. In such circumstances, it is likely to be extremely difficult to obtain warranties and indemnities; indeed, even if available, there is likely to be a question mark over whether funds would be available to meet any such liabilities. The danger of unseen liabilities is such that a share sale will rarely be contemplated in such circumstances and there would be an obvious attraction in seeking to structure the transaction so as to avoid the application of TUPE. However, this is likely to be difficult to achieve, particularly if the purchaser wishes to continue to operate the business in a similar manner.

As a result, the purchaser has a limited number of options in attempting to cap his exposure to unseen liabilities:

- Attempt to identify any liabilities and seek a reduction in the purchase price in order to compensate.
- Undertake more extensive due diligence.
- Avoid the application of TUPE if at all possible.

Given that the transferor will invariably offer no future for the employees and will have no resources to meet employment-related liabilities, the employees are likely to argue on any sale of all or part of the business that their employment and all associated liabilities have transferred to the transferee. There will be TUPE issues to be considered where there is a sale of shares, if the hive-down model is adopted (see diagram below).

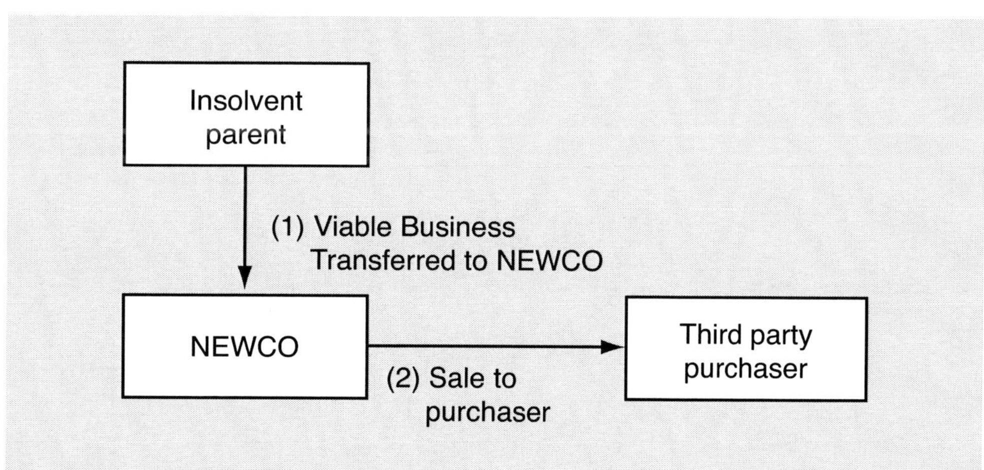

In order to make businesses in financial difficulty more attractive to potential purchasers, TUPE contains provisions whereby in certain circumstances accrued employee liabilities will be met by the State and – to that extent – will not pass to the purchaser. The scope of the payments which are protected is based on the entitlement in respect of redundancies and other payments which are covered by the State on an insolvency. Additionally, the ability of the purchaser to change terms and conditions is increased by contrast to the ordinary rules within TUPE. Sadly, this is an area where the law is less than clear and the provisions of Regulation 8 of TUPE will have to be considered carefully in the context of each insolvency situation. For example, the Guidance issued by the Redundancy Payments Office and the decision of the Employment Appeal Tribunal in *Oakland v Wellswood (Yorkshire) Ltd* (EAT 395/08) conflict as to whether 'prepack' administrations are covered by these provisions.

Chapter 4
TUPE – consequences and effects

- Overview
- Who transfers?
- What transfers?
- Dismissals

Chapter 4
TUPE – consequences and effects

Overview

The principal implications of TUPE may be summarised in general terms as follows:

- Employees working immediately before the transfer in the business being sold become employees of the purchaser.
- Terms and conditions of employment transfer, save in respect of certain terms relating to occupational pension schemes.
- Liabilities in relation to transferring employees transfer to the purchaser.
- Dismissals connected with the transfer are automatically unfair unless made for an economic, technical or organisational reason.
- Collective agreements in respect of transferring employees transfer.
- Union recognition may transfer, dependent upon whether the business being transferred retains its identity post-transfer.
- An obligation to inform and (in certain circumstances) to consult with employee representatives arises.

Who transfers?

Regulation 4(1) of TUPE provides that:

> '… a relevant transfer shall not operate so as to terminate the contract of employment of any person employed by the transferor and assigned to the organised grouping of resources or employees that is subject to the relevant transfer, which would otherwise have been terminated by the transfer, but any such contract shall have effect after the transfer as if originally made between the person so employed and the transferee.'

Hence, for there to be a transfer of a contract of employment to the purchaser, that person must:

- Be employed (and this would exclude someone engaged under a contract for services);
- By the transferor; and
- Be assigned to the target.

Particular care needs to be taken when dealing with groups of companies. Consider the following situation:

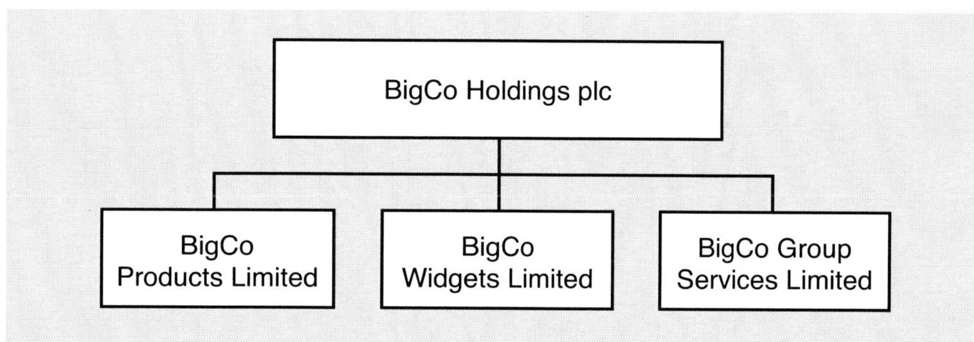

It is not uncommon for a group of companies to be structured so that all of its employees are employed through a service company. If all the employees working in BigCo Products Limited were employed by BigCo Group Services Limited and BigCo Products Limited sold one of its businesses, arguably none of those employees would transfer to the purchaser because they would not be employed by the transferor (i.e. BigCo Products Limited) but by a third party (i.e. BigCo Group Services Limited).

It is particularly important to take into account these issues when undertaking due diligence. In order to attempt to transfer the workforce in these circumstances, BigCo Group Services Limited should be joined in as a party to the transaction so that it becomes a transferor. There is still a question as to whether or not the mere transfer of the provision of employees can of itself amount to the transfer of an undertaking so as to fall within TUPE. The case of *Barclays Bank plc v Banking Insurance and Finance Union* [1987] ICR 495 suggests that there would not be a transfer in these circumstances. Having said that, it is felt by many that in the light of the decision of the European Court in *Schmidt* (supra), *Barclays Bank* would now be decided differently. Moreover, the transfer of staff may be seen as a constituent part of the transfer of the undertaking as a whole and it is quite likely that joining BigCo Group Services Limited as a party in such circumstances would be sufficient to achieve a transfer of the employees under TUPE. Encouragement is given to this line of reasoning by the decision of the Employment Appeal Tribunal in *Duncan Web Offset (Maidstone) v Cooper* [1995] IRLR 633 in which the court drew attention to this gap in the application of TUPE where groups of companies were involved and vowed not to allow it to become exploited as a way of avoiding the implications of TUPE. Once again, however, this is an area of uncertainty.

The question of whether an employee will transfer may also arise if they are only partially employed in the target. Let us suppose, for example, that a company has four department stores in a city centre and the maintenance department is staffed by four employees. The employees work as a team covering the four stores; the balance of the time which each employee spends in each store may be summarised as follows:

	Smith	**Jones**	**Brown**	**Green**
Store A	0	75%	5%	50%
Store B	20%	25%	10	0%
Store C	5%	0	75%	50%
Store D	75%	0	10%	0

The decision of the European Court in *Botzen v Rotterdamsche Droogdok Maatschapij* [1986] 2 CMLR 50 stated that, where employees are partially engaged in the undertaking which transfers and partially engaged elsewhere, the question of whether or not they transfer with the undertaking depends on whether or not they are 'assigned' to the transferring undertaking or part of an undertaking. In practice, this is not always easy to determine. In the absence of a formal assignment, it is likely to be implied where an employee is spending a substantial amount of his time on behalf of the transferring undertaking or part of an undertaking. There is no definitive guidance available on what percentage of working time might be sufficient to amount to an assignment for these purposes.

If Store B was sold, it is unlikely that any of the maintenance staff would transfer. Clearly, Store B has lower maintenance requirements than the other stores, and although three of the four staff work at Store B, none of them devote much of their time to that store. If Store B was sold, therefore, the purchaser would have to make arrangements for the maintenance of Store B post-transfer such as deploying existing staff to the maintenance of Store B or recruiting. This could include making an offer of employment to someone such as Jones. The purchaser would be free to offer whatever terms and conditions it wanted. Jones's continuity of employment would not be transferred. If the purchaser does not take on any of the maintenance staff, the maintenance department serving the remaining three stores of the vendor would be overstaffed to the extent of approximately one half an employee. It will be appreciated that in circumstances where there are significant numbers of employees in this situation, the potential redundancy costs and the staffing implications are considerable.

If Store C was to be sold, both Brown and Green could transfer to the purchaser. Brown spends the greater part of his time at Store C and only a small amount of time at each of the other stores. Green's position is far less clear – he splits his time equally between Store A and Store C. If Brown and Green both transfer, it would mean that the vendor has taken more maintenance staff than the target requires – two employees for work that only justified a head count of 1.3. If Green did not transfer, the vendor would be overstaffed and the purchaser would have inherited a workforce lighter than needed.

In practice, these issues are encountered frequently and there are no clear answers. There is considerable scope for negotiation, given that there is a balance to be struck between adequate staffing and potential redundancy costs. Hence the importance of the list in the sale and purchase agreement of those employees transferring to the purchaser. This list will frequently be the subject of negotiation. A pragmatic solution of this nature needs the cooperation of the employees, who always have the right to go to a tribunal and to claim that the correct legal principles have not been applied when determining their fate.

Immediately before the transfer

In order to be transferred to the purchaser by TUPE, the employee must be employed by the transferor immediately before the transfer. This raises the prospect of dismissals and rearrangements being effected at the eleventh hour.

Certainly, the possibility of 'rearranging the furniture' should not be overlooked; a vendor may well move a valued employee out of the target (pursuant to a mobility clause in his contract of employment or by agreement) in order that he may be retained. Equally, employees from elsewhere in the vendor's operations who are surplus to requirements may be moved into the target in order that the vendor may rid himself of such employees without having to make severance payments. To some extent this can be spotted by careful due diligence and by scrutiny of the list of transferring employees. It may not be possible, however, for the purchaser to spot such a move and in such circumstances the purchaser will have to rely on warranties – for example, a warranty that all transferring employees have been working in their current jobs for at least six months before the date of transfer.

Where dismissals are effected shortly before the transfer then, following the 'purposive' interpretation of TUPE by the House of Lords in *Litster v Forth Estuary Engineering* [1989] IRLR 161, if the dismissal was effected in connection with the transfer, the liability to pay compensation will pass to the purchaser, as will any other liabilities relating to that employee.

Knowledge of the transfer

It is not necessary that an employee who would otherwise be covered by TUPE is aware of the transfer taking place. The point has been open to doubt as a result of conflicting case law, but now appears to have been settled by the case of *Secretary of State for Employment v Cook* [1997] IRLR 150.

It is necessary to take care, when undertaking due diligence, in respect of employees who may be away from work on an extended basis, absent sick or on maternity leave. Such employees may transfer under TUPE even though the purchaser does not know of their existence and even though the employee may be unaware that the transaction has taken place.

The employee's right to refuse to transfer

By virtue of Regulation 4(7) of TUPE, an employee may opt out of transferring to the purchaser on the grounds that he objects to becoming employed by the transferee. However, the contract of employment merely comes to an end in these circumstances without the need for ordinary notice to be given under the contract; the employee has no entitlement to claim that he has been unfairly dismissed if he leaves in such circumstances and he has no entitlement to a redundancy payment. If an employee is crucial to the purchaser, the purchaser should be aware of the danger of the employee leaving in these circumstances and should consider what to put into the sale and purchase agreement to cover the situation should the key employee decide to exercise this option.

This Regulation holds out the possibility of an organised refusal to transfer. For example, a trade union may coordinate a threat by each employee to exercise the option not to transfer if a transaction goes ahead on certain terms. This could have the consequence of frustrating the transfer in circumstances where the transfer of such employees was considered essential by the purchaser. It remains to be seen whether such a weapon will be used by trade unions.

There are two other circumstances where an employee may refuse to transfer. There is always the option of resigning and claiming constructive dismissal – a claim which could potentially be brought against either the vendor or the purchaser, depending on the circumstances. Additionally, an employee can resign when the transfer will involve a substantial change in his working conditions to his material detriment. No entitlement to notice pay arises in these circumstances, but the resignation will amount to a dismissal and hence it will be open to the employee to bring a claim of constructive dismissal.

What transfers?

Regulation 4(2)(a) of TUPE states that 'all the transferor's rights, powers, duties and liabilities under or in connection with' the transferring employee's contract of employment are transferred to the transferee.

This is an all-embracing concept that includes:

- Rights under the contract of employment;
- Statutory rights; and
- Continuity of employment.

Rights which transfer include:

a. *Terms and Conditions*: employees formerly employed by the vendor in the target become employees of the transferee on the same terms and conditions. To a large extent, it is as if a contract of employment had been pulled from the personnel records and the name of the employer changed to the purchaser: a sort of statutory novation.

   One of the respects in which TUPE not only protects but enhances the acquired rights of the employees is emphasised by the case of *Wilson v St. Helen's Borough Council* [1998] IRLR 706, which held that an attempt to change terms and conditions of employment in connection with the transfer, regardless of whether or not the changes were made with the consent of the employee, will be void. The situation is now governed by Regulation 4(4) of TUPE. It is important to be aware that, when purchasing a business, the purchaser will be bound by those terms and conditions, at least for the medium term. The situation should be contrasted with an acquisition by way of shares, where there is no such prohibition on changing terms and conditions. It may well be that, where the purchaser proposes to integrate the target into an existing business, he will want to harmonise terms and conditions of employment across the new enlarged business. However, he is significantly restricted in what he is at liberty to do, unless he is prepared to dismiss the employees following the transfer and to re-engage them on different terms. This issue is discussed in greater detail in chapter 6.

b. *Status*: the employment relationship is transferred as if the employee had always been employed by the purchaser. Hence, any status-related benefits would also transfer – for example, holiday entitlement which is calculated by length of service would be calculated on the basis of continuity of service stretching back before the transfer. Equally, seniority is capable of transferring.

c. *Arrears of pay*: because there is a transfer of the employment relationship and of all associated liabilities, any contractual arrears will transfer. For example, if there are arrears of pay, outstanding expenses or accrued benefits such as holiday pay, these will all transfer. Needless to say, it is important for the purchaser to either quantify these outstanding liabilities and to anticipate them when settling on a purchase price or to take an indemnity. The latter is the appropriate course of action, assuming that the transferor is credit worthy for the indemnity, and it is for this reason that an indemnity, specifically directed towards anticipated liabilities, is appropriate even though it may be difficult to take other protection within the sale and purchase agreement on an indemnity basis.

d. *Statutory claims*: statutory rights will transfer in tandem with contractual rights. This will mean, for example, that an employee who has been employed by the transferee for only a matter of months may have the right to bring a claim for unfair dismissal against the purchaser shortly after the transfer because of the aggregation of his pre-transfer service. The date of commencement of continuous service will be the date that applied in relation to employment with the vendor.

e. *Restrictive covenants*: as contract terms, restrictive covenants will transfer. It is to be noted, however, that the extent to which they are appropriate must be reviewed by the purchaser. For example, the restrictions may relate to various group operations of the vendor. Those may be of little relevance to the purchaser and the purchaser may wish to take protection in relation to other aspects of his group with which the employee will have contact. Therefore it will be necessary to consider putting new restrictive covenants into place. The vendor should also bear in mind that he will lose the protection of restrictive covenants, for the benefit of the covenants will transfer to become a contractual benefit for the purchaser. There is a difficulty here if the vendor is particularly concerned to retain protection after the transfer and the vendor should, therefore, consider putting in place new covenants which will survive the transfer. An added complication is that a change in terms and conditions of employment in connection with a TUPE transfer is void. The point was well illustrated in *Credit Suisse First Boston (Europe) Ltd v Lister* [1998] IRLR 700. Hence an independent rationale will have to be found for the introduction of new covenants.

f. *Share options*: share option rights are capable of transferring as a matter of theory but in practice the rules of share option schemes will generally be drafted so that the right to participate ceases to exist upon the employee ceasing to be employed by the vendor. It is possible (but will rarely be encountered) that the employee may have a right which is capable of being construed so that it gives clear rights enforceable against the purchaser.

g. *Bonuses and profit sharing*: again, these rights are capable of transferring as a matter of theory, but often the criteria for the award of such benefits will have changed by reason of the transfer. For example, a bonus may be awarded referable to the performance of a larger unit than the unit which was transferred. If the scheme does not specifically provide for what should happen upon a transfer, then it may be that the transferee is put in a position where the scheme itself has transferred but is not capable of operating in the post-transfer environment. The rules of the scheme itself would have to be considered to see if provision is made for such circumstances. In order to avoid a breach of contract, the purchaser may have to put into place a benefit of equivalent value.

h. *Industrial injuries*: an industrial injury claim will transfer. Hence, the purchaser could find itself liable for substantial claims where, for example, employees were exposed, pre-transfer, to a harmful working environment. Particular attention should be given by the purchaser to insurance cover in place in respect of such claims pre-transfer. A transferee employee will be entitled to rely on the insurance policy of the transferor in respect of transferring employees: see *Bernadone v Pall Mall Services Group* [2002] IRLR 487. In certain circumstances, the industrial injury claim will not transfer but will be a joint and several liability of the transferor and the transferee (see Regulation 17 of TUPE). Typically, the purchaser will in any event seek a warranty in respect of claims originating prior to the transfer date.

This draws attention to the need for purchasers to undertake an HR audit as soon as possible after the transfer to assess the workforce which has been inherited. It is necessary for the HR management of the purchaser to 'hit the ground running' so that HR issues which surface shortly after the transfer are seen in the context of a continuing employment relationship. For example, if an employee has been subjected to stress at work and is on the point of a nervous breakdown at the time of the transfer, the purchaser should not expect to be given any period of grace post-transfer.

A similar situation arises in relation to discipline. For example, an employee may be in the course of disciplinary proceedings at the time of transfer, or some aspect of that employee's performance may be in the course of being monitored. Those proceedings or that monitoring procedure must continue uninterrupted.

The following do not transfer:

a. *Pensions*: rights in relation to occupational pension schemes are specifically excluded from the scope of TUPE by Regulation 10. The following points, however, should be borne in mind:

   - It is only rights in relation to occupational pension schemes that do not transfer. If, for example, there was a clause in an employee's contract of employment whereby his employer was obliged to pay 5 per cent of salary into a personal pension plan on behalf of that employee, then such a right would not be a right in relation to an occupational pension scheme and would transfer.

   - It is only the provisions of an occupational pension scheme that relate to old age, invalidity or survivors that will not transfer. If, for example, there is a severance benefit scheme built into the pension scheme, then this would transfer. Early retirement rights are likewise transferable (see *Beckmann* [2002] IRLR 578).

   - Where the transferor provided occupational pension scheme benefits, the transferee employer will be required to offer pension benefits to a certain level, although there is no obligation to match the level of pension benefits to which the employee was entitled pre-transfer. The transferor will be required to match employer contributions up to 6 per cent of pensionable salary in a stakeholder scheme or provide a suitable equivalent.

b. *Criminal liability*: does not transfer.

c. *Vicarious liability*: whereby the employer becomes liable for non-employment law claims arising from the acts of the employee done in the course of his employment, does not transfer.

Dismissals

The impact of TUPE is to preserve continuity of employment and therefore such rights as an employee has in relation to unfair dismissal are retained, notwithstanding the transfer and change of employer. Although it was at one stage considered (see *Milligan v Securicor Cleaning* [1995] IRLR 288) that the statutory qualification period which is ordinarily applicable in unfair dismissal cases had no application where the dismissal was by reason of a transfer, this misconception was corrected by the *Collective Redundancies and Transfer of Undertakings (Protection of Employment) (Amendment) Regulations 1995* (SI 1995/2587).

Where an employee is dismissed and the reason for dismissal relates to the transfer, additional rights are given to an employee by virtue of Regulation 7 of TUPE, which provides that the dismissal will be automatically unfair in certain circumstances:

> '(1) Where either before or after a relevant transfer, any employee of the transferor or transferee is dismissed, that employee shall be treated ... as unfairly dismissed if the sole or principal reason for his dismissal is:
>
> (a) the transfer itself; or
>
> (b) a reason connected with the transfer that is not an economic, technical or organisational reason entailing changes in the workforce.'

Hence this is a two stage process. A reason for dismissal which arises from the very fact of the transfer will be automatically unfair. A reason which is transfer-related, but which is one stage removed from the transfer (such as, for example, a post-transfer reorganisation to incorporate the target into the purchaser's group) is potentially automatically unfair, depending on whether there is an 'ETO reason'.

The presumption of unfairness is rebutted 'where the sole or principal reason for the dismissal is a reason connected with the transfer that is an economic, technical or organisational reason entailing changes in the workforce of either the transferor or the transferee before or after a relevant transfer.'

Where a dismissal is found to be automatically unfair, the only question for the employment tribunal will be to decide what remedy would be appropriate.

The only defences open to an employer against a claim of this nature are to argue that the dismissal is not, in fact, connected with the transfer or, if this defence is unsuccessful, that this is a dismissal for an economic, technical or organisational reason. However, even if this defence succeeds, it only avoids the dismissal being considered automatically unfair and the employer must still defend the case along the ordinary lines of an unfair dismissal claim.

The question is often asked whether there is any rule of thumb as to how much time must elapse between the transfer and the dismissal in order for a dismissal not to be considered as being connected with the transfer. In fact, there is no rule of thumb. Certainly, the longer the period, the more difficult it is likely to be for an employee to link the transfer with the dismissal, but it is not the period of time that is the key factor here, but whether or not there is any causal link.

The economic, technical or organisational reason ('ETO') defence is not defined in TUPE and there is limited case law on the subject. However, the approach of the employment tribunal will generally be that if there has been a considered decision to dismiss based on genuine business reasons that arose at the time of the dismissal, the ETO defence will be established, thereby leaving the case to be dealt with on its merits as an ordinary unfair dismissal or redundancy case. 'Economic' might be something that arises from the business itself such as a loss of a major contract. 'Organisational' could be taking out a layer of middle management. 'Technical' could be the need to utilise different equipment needing materially different skills. The 'ETO reason' must entail a change in the workforce: this is taken to mean a change in numbers or a change in function.

Although either the transferor or the transferee can rely on the ETO defence, the courts have been very careful not to allow the 'economic' defence to encompass dismissals at the request or direction of the transferee, or dismissals pre-transfer for the purpose of making the target more attractive for a purchaser. For example, in *Wheeler v Patel* [1987] ICR 631, the EAT held that dismissals so as to make the target more attractive, thereby securing a better price, did not relate to the 'conduct' of the business and hence did not fall within the scope of the ETO defence.

It would appear that there is some scope for pre-transfer dismissals whilst at the same time avoiding automatically unfair dismissals. This arises from the question of whether the dismissal must, in order to be automatically unfair, relate to a particular transfer or to contemplation of a transfer generally. In *Longden v Ferrari* [1994] IRLR 157, the dismissal took place in contemplation of the sale generally but not (on the evidence) of a specific sale. Hence the dismissals were held not to be in contemplation of the transfer that ultimately took place and therefore not to be automatically unfair.

It is clear that dismissals in such circumstances are particularly dangerous. In planning for the costs associated with the transfer, both the vendor and the purchaser should assume a significant risk of unfair dismissal liability if dismissals are likely to be occasioned in connection with the transfer. It is common in such circumstances for the cost of dismissals to be taken into account when negotiating a price and for indemnities (typically up to a certain limit) to be agreed anticipating dismissal liabilities.

The transfer itself cannot be treated as a dismissal. If the purchaser simply refused to employ the transferring employees, this would be treated as a dismissal by the purchaser.

One issue of concern to the employees of vendors and purchasers alike is whether, in the event that redundancies are necessary as a result of the transfer, the selection of those candidates for redundancy must be from the employees of the purchaser as well as the transferring employees or whether the 'pool' is limited to the employees in the transferring business. There is no clear answer to this question but the purchaser should be aware that there is a danger that redundancies may be unfair by reason of unfairness within the selection process if candidates for redundancy are not selected from both groups and there are no good objective reasons for selecting from one group only.

Chapter 5
Information and consultation

- Share sales
- Asset sales: TUPE Regulations 13-16
- Transfer of union recognition and collective agreements
- Vendor's checklist
- Purchaser's checklist

Chapter 5
Information and consultation

Share sales

Whilst informing employees and their representatives of the nature of M & A proposals and consulting with them about the consequences of those proposals may be seen as desirable in terms of good HR management practice, the obligations are materially greater in business sales than in share sales. Indeed, there may be no legal obligation to inform or to consult where the transaction is to be effected by way of a share sale. There is no general obligation to inform and consult, although a duty will arise in certain circumstances. For example, a works council may be in place and a duty to consult may arise under the *Information and Consultation of Employees Regulations 2004*. However, where TUPE applies the duty to inform always arises and a duty to consult will arise in most cases.

More often than not, negotiations will be conducted confidentially. Sensitivity as to the impact of the proposed transaction on the workforce of the target will often be one reason for such secrecy. The absence of a legal obligation to disclose information to employees and their representatives where the transaction is to be effected by way of a share sale leaves the way open for complete flexibility of strategy and is to be contrasted with the obligations that arise under TUPE, described below.

In practice, the parties to a share sale transaction will need to take into account the broader industrial relations consequences of failing to divulge information and of failing to consult with employees and their representatives. Certainly, the mere fact that the transaction is to be effected by way of a share sale rather than an asset sale is unlikely to mean that these are not issues of considerable concern about which employees and their representatives might wish to be informed and about which they might wish to be consulted. The parties will also have to consider whether any other obligations to inform and to consult arise, such as under the terms of a collective agreement.

If redundancies will be declared as a result of or in conjunction with the transfer, additional obligations to inform and to consult with employee representatives may arise – see page 62.

Asset sales: TUPE Regulations 13-16

Where TUPE applies there are significant legal obligations to disclose information and to consult. These are set out in Regulation 13 of TUPE.

Who is subject to the duty?

Both the vendor and the purchaser may have obligations, although the principal obligations rest with the vendor.

The obligations set out in Regulation 13 of TUPE concern 'affected employees'; in order to establish the extent of the duty to inform and to consult it is necessary to identify which affected employees fall within that definition. The definition is set out in Regulation 13(1) as:

> 'any employees of the transferor or the transferee (whether or not assigned to the organised grouping of resources or employees that is the subject of a relevant transfer) who may be affected by the transfer or may be affected by measures taken in connection with it...'

Hence any employees in the following categories may be the subject of a duty under Regulation 13:

a. Employees of the vendor who are employed in the undertaking or the part of the undertaking to be transferred.

b. Other employees of the vendor regardless of their connection with the undertaking being transferred.

c. Employees of the purchaser.

The test is whether or not any such employee 'may be affected by the transfer or may be affected by measures taken in connection with it'. Employees in (a) will inevitably fall within the duty in Regulation 13, even if only because the identity of their employer will change as a result of the transfer. Employees in (b) and (c) may also fall within the definition, depending upon the circumstances of each case.

The 'may be affected' test allows for a degree of subjectivity, but in practice an employer should bear in mind that if there is a real possibility that any employee falling within one of the above three categories will be affected by the transfer or by measures taken in connection with it, the employer may be in breach of his Regulation 13 duty if he fails to include that employee within the information and consultation process.

What is the employer obliged to do?

The duty is comprised of two stages:

a. An obligation to inform employee representatives; and

b. (In certain circumstances) an obligation to follow the disclosure of information with a process of consultation with employee representatives.

Information

The information which an employer of an affected employee is bound to disclose is set out in Regulation 13(2) of TUPE as follows:

a. The fact that the relevant transfer is to take place; when, approximately, it is to take place and the reasons for it; and

b. The legal, economic and social implications of the transfer for the affected employees; and

c. The measures which he envisages he will, in connection with the transfer, take in relation to those employees or, if he envisages that no measures will be so taken, that fact; and

d. If the employer is the vendor, the measures which the purchaser envisages he will, in connection with the transfer, take in relation to such of those employees as, by virtue of Regulation 4 of TUPE, become employees of the purchaser after the transfer or, if he envisages that no measures will be so taken, that fact.

This obligation is most often encountered in circumstances where the vendor is obliged to inform employee representatives in the context of an impending sale of the business. However, it will be appreciated from the above that the purchaser may also have a duty to inform. Even if the purchaser has no obligation to consult with its own workforce, the purchaser has an obligation, set out in Regulation 13(4) of TUPE, to pass to the vendor the information that the vendor will need to comply with its obligation in Regulation 13(2)(d). The consequences of a failure by the purchaser to deliver that information to the vendor at such a time as to enable the vendor to comply with its obligations are explained on page 62.

A precedent for use in connection with the disclosure of information may be found at page 108.

When to inform

The obligation to disclose information is to make disclosures 'long enough before a relevant transfer to enable the employer of any affected employees to consult all the persons who are appropriate representatives of any of those affected employees…'.

As will be explained below, the obligation to consult does not arise in every case where there is an obligation to inform; the timescale for the disclosure of information is nevertheless set by reference to consultation. Accordingly, there is an argument that, if there is no obligation to consult, the information may be delivered at the eleventh hour in advance of a transfer being effected, given that even such short notice would still be long enough where there is no obligation to consult.

Where there is an obligation to consult, then it will be a matter of judgment in each case as to how long is needed for consultation, depending on the issues that are on the agenda. In practice, the earlier that the employer feels able to commence the information and consultation process, the less the likelihood of falling foul of Regulation 13 of TUPE.

It is self evident on the wording of Regulation 13(2)(a) of TUPE that there is no requirement to inform until it is clear that there will be a transfer. The obligation to inform does not arise merely as a result of proposals or mere possibilities. In *NATTKE v Rank Leisure* (COIT 1388/134) the tribunal held that the duty arose when there was a binding agreement in place or when it becomes evident beyond doubt that the transfer will take place. The former test may work in circumstances where there is deferred completion but does not work when there is simultaneous contract and completion. In practice, once it becomes likely that the transaction will go ahead, the duty to inform and to consult will become ever more pressing.

Who to inform

The obligation is to inform and, where appropriate, to consult with 'appropriate representatives' of the affected employees. These representatives may fall into one of two categories, namely:

- Employee representatives elected by the employees either for the specific purpose of receiving information and being consulted, or in circumstances where it is appropriate for them to act in these circumstances (for example, members of a staff council);

- Trade union representatives, where an independent trade union is recognised by the employer in respect of employees of that description.

Where there is a recognised union, the trade union representatives will be the appropriate representatives. If there is no recognised trade union, the representatives will be – at the choice of the employer – newly elected representatives or representatives already in place who are authorised to act in this capacity. The situation will often arise where there are no such representatives to whom to disclose information and with whom to consult. In such circumstances an employer can escape the duty to inform and to consult if:

- He invites the affected employees to elect representatives;
- He does so leaving enough time for both the election and the information/consultation process to take place

and yet no employees are elected.

How to inform

Regulation 13(5) of TUPE provides a choice:

- Delivering the information to the representatives; or
- Sending it by post to an address given to the employer by the representatives; or
- (In the case of union representatives) sending it by post to the head or main office of the union.

Consultation

The duty to consult will arise in some, but not all, of the cases covered by the duty to inform. It is described in Regulation 13(6) of TUPE:

> 'An employer of an affected employee who envisages that he will take measures in relation to an affected employee, in connection with the relevant transfer, shall consult the appropriate representatives of that employee with a view to seeking their agreement to the intended measures.'

The key tests are frustratingly vague:

- 'Envisages': the exact degree of foresight and certainty of planning is not defined.
- 'Measures': such judicial assistance as there is (e.g. *IPCS v Sec. of State for Defence* [1987] IRLR 71: 'any action, step or arrangement') is of limited

value. Any change to employment terms or working arrangements, however material, would appear to be capable of triggering this duty. It may not take very much for a tribunal to conclude that 'measures' are envisaged: see *Todd v Strain (EATS/0057/10)*.

What is meant by consultation?

It is clear from Regulation 13(7) of TUPE that the employer must:

- Consider any representations made by the representatives.
- Reply to those representations.
- State his reasons if he rejects any of those representations.
- Allow sufficient time for a meaningful consultation exercise, depending on the circumstances of each case.

The employer will need to show some sense of purpose, for he is to consult with a view to reaching agreement.

The employer is obliged to allow the representatives access to the affected employees and to provide such accommodation and other facilities as may be appropriate.

The Special Circumstances Defence

Regulation 13(9) of TUPE provides that, where there are special circumstances which render it not reasonably practicable for an employer to perform any aspect of the duty to inform or to consult, he shall take all such steps toward performing that duty as are reasonably practicable in the circumstances.

The exact scope of this defence remains unclear. Much will depend on the particular circumstances of each case. However, it is clear that insolvency per se cannot amount to a special circumstance: see *Clarks of Hove Ltd v Bakers Union* [1978] IRLR 366, where insolvency occurred as a result of the gradual run-down of the company. A sudden and catastrophic downturn in business, by contrast, could justify a failure to conform with the obligations to inform and to consult.

Note that there is in any event an obligation to take all steps to comply with the obligations to inform and to consult as are reasonably practicable in the circumstances.

The practical advice is to conform to the obligations wherever possible, leaving the special circumstances defence as very much a last resort.

Remedies

It is primarily the employee representatives who have a direct remedy against an employer who fails to inform or to consult. The employees themselves are, to a large extent, left with an indirect remedy.

Applications should be made to an employment tribunal. There is a time limit of three months which begins from the date of the transfer.

The remedy is exclusively financial. An injunction will not be granted to delay the transfer going ahead where there is inadequate information disclosed or a failure to consult (see *Betts v Brintel Helicopters* [1996] IRLR 45).

The remedy is a maximum of thirteen weeks pay for each employee depending on the seriousness of the employer's breach. The statutory limit on the value of a week's pay does not apply for these purposes.

Where an employer is precluded from disclosing the information required to be disclosed by Regulation 13(2)(d) of TUPE because the purchaser did not disclose the information to the vendor in time, the purchaser may be joined into any proceedings brought against the vendor arising from that alleged failure. An award of compensation may be made directly against the purchaser.

It is normal for a purchaser of a business to build in to the sale and purchase agreement an acknowledgement from the vendor that the information required from the vendor has been received together with an undertaking not to serve a notice under Regulation 15(5) of TUPE joining the purchaser into any tribunal proceedings.

Redundancies

Care should be taken not to overlook the laws applicable to employers proposing to declare redundancies. If redundancies are to be occasioned by reason of or in conjunction with the transfer, whether a share transfer or an assets transfer, the consultation and notification requirements of the *Trade Union and Labour Relations (Consolidation) Act 1992 (as amended by the Trade Union Reform and Employment Rights Act 1993)* must be considered. These may be summarised as:

a. If there is a proposal to dismiss 20 or more employees by reason of redundancy at one establishment within a 90 day period, the Redundancy Payments Service must be notified.

b. Any such proposal must also be the subject of consultation with 'appropriate representatives' of the employees.

c. Consultation must be accompanied by the disclosure of certain information.

d. a 30 day consultation period must be made available for dismissals of 20 or more within 90 days; 90 days must be made available for dismissals of 100 or more within 90 days.

If redundancies are to be declared, the employer will have responsibilities at a collective and individual level which are a topic in their own right upon which advice should be sought.

Transfer of union recognition and collective agreements

Not only does TUPE have the effect of transferring the terms and conditions of employment of employees engaged in an undertaking, collective agreements and union recognition relating to such employees may also transfer.

Transfer of trade union recognition

Under Regulation 6 of TUPE, where the undertaking which has been transferred maintains an identity post-transfer which is distinct from the remainder of the purchaser's undertaking, then trade union recognition rights are capable of being transferred to the purchaser. Where an independent trade union is recognised by the vendor in respect of employees who become employees of the purchaser by operation of TUPE, then the purchaser shall be deemed to have recognised the union to the same extent as recognition was granted by the vendor.

Transfer of collective agreements

The transfer of collective agreements relating to transferring employees is occasioned by Regulation 5 of TUPE, which provides that:

a. Where at the time of the transfer there is a collective agreement in place

b. Which has been made by or on behalf of the vendor (that is to say that it would encompass a collective agreement where the vendor participates through a trade association)

c. With a trade union recognised by the vendor in respect of any employee whose contract transfers to the purchaser by reason of the application of TUPE Regulation 4, then in such circumstances that collective agreement applies in relation to that employee as if made by the purchaser.

Unless expressly stated to the contrary, collective agreements are presumed not to be legally binding and invariably state that they have no legal effect. Regulation 5 of TUPE is therefore of limited significance.

The consequences of a transfer of collective agreements, however, should not be underestimated. The purchaser may well find that having persistently rejected attempts by a trade union to obtain recognition, recognition comes in through the back door by reason of an acquisition covered by TUPE. Industrial relations consequences may be supplemented by legal consequences if and when a legal framework of mandatory recognition of trade unions is reintroduced.

Vendor's checklist

1. Is the transaction a share sale or an asset sale to which TUPE does not apply? If so, check obligations under any collective agreements or works council constitutions or under the Takeover Code. Otherwise, whether to inform and consult is a matter for management discretion.
2. If the transaction is governed by TUPE, identify all affected employees.
3. Request from the purchaser information as to whether the purchaser envisages he will take any measures in relation to the transferring employees.
4. Consider whether there is a recognised trade union: if there is, they must be informed. If there is not, consider whether to use an existing body or to invite employees to elect representatives.
5. Deliver information.
6. Consider whether a duty to consult arises.
7. Compile information and deliver to representatives allowing sufficient time for any consultation which may be necessary.
8. Consult where necessary.

Purchaser's checklist

1. If the transaction is governed by TUPE identify all affected employees.
2. Consider what measures will be taken in relation to the transferring employees and convey this information to the vendor.
3. Consider whether measures are being taken in respect of any of the purchaser's existing employees – if the answer is 'yes', follow the procedures as for the vendor above.

Chapter 6
Absorbing the target

- Harmonisation
- Practical steps
- Notifying employees of a change of employer

Chapter 6
Absorbing the target

Harmonisation

Following the acquisition, a purchaser will often wish to change the terms and conditions of employment of those engaged in the target. There is a considerable difference here between the rules that would apply where the acquisition is governed by TUPE, and the rules that apply in circumstances where a transaction is not governed by TUPE, for example on the acquisition of shares.

Where TUPE does not apply, it may be that the purchaser will be in a position simply to recruit the employees formerly engaged by the transferor in the business, and the purchaser will be free to do so on the open employment market. Harmonisation of terms will not be a problem in such circumstances as the purchaser may recruit on his own standard terms.

Where the purchaser has acquired the workforce by reason of the acquisition of shares, then any changes in terms and conditions, for example in order to bring the terms and conditions of the employees in the target in line with the purchaser's group as a whole, will be dealt with in accordance with the rules that would have applied had there not been a change of ownership. The employer must ensure that terms and conditions are either changed by agreement or changed on notice, so as not to give rise to a wrongful dismissal claim. In order to avoid the danger of an unfair dismissal claim, the employer must have sound business reasons for wanting to change terms and conditions, must consult with the employees and must seek to reach an agreement by consent. Only where those efforts have been made would it be appropriate to introduce a change (see *Hollister v National Farmer's Union* [1979] ICR 542). The fact that there has been a change of ownership may well be taken into account in the assessment of whether or not there are sound business reasons behind the change.

Where TUPE applies, the employer's options are more restricted. This is largely a consequence of the decision in *Wilson v St. Helen's Borough Council* (supra). In that case, a number of teachers and carers who worked at a home run by the County Council were made redundant when the local authority ceded control of the home. The Borough Council immediately assumed control and some of the employees were offered the same positions on less favourable terms and conditions. The employees did not formally accept the new terms but did not object to them either. They worked under the new contracts before making any objection to the variation of their terms and conditions. It was held that there was a transfer under TUPE; any variation of terms between the new employer and staff as a result of the transfer was overridden by TUPE and hence the contract terms in force before the transfer were upheld.

The law was codified and revised in the 2006 revision of TUPE. Employers are not free to renegotiate terms and conditions with staff about to be transferred in an attempt to make the target more attractive, nor are transferee employers free to renegotiate the terms and conditions. Hence the purchaser, where TUPE applies, may be unable to achieve a harmonisation of terms and conditions. Any change to terms and conditions will be void if made as a consequence of the transfer. Any change which is for a reason connected with the transfer will be void if the reason is not an economic, technical or organisational reason entailing changes in the workforce. The latter phrase can be particularly difficult to accommodate in many cases..

In practical terms, therefore, the purchaser must anticipate that he may well not be free to vary terms and conditions. The longer the amount of time that lapses between the transfer and the variation, the more difficult it is likely to be to establish a connection. Harmonisation may be introduced as part of a broader review of terms related to the group as a whole, not simply the target. The danger is that not only will harmonisation be invalid, but if a dismissal occurs (which could be a constructive dismissal) any termination of employment by reason of the transfer will be automatically unfair unless the employer is able to establish the economic, technical or organisational reason defence.

The one exception to these principles is in the case of rescues of insolvent companies, where changes may be permitted provided that the employee representatives consent. The detail of these provisions may be found in Regulation 9 of TUPE.

Practical steps

Clearly, the purchaser's post-acquisition strategy will vary from target to target, but one factor that is common is the assumption of responsibility for HR management by the purchaser. It is essential that the purchaser anticipates this management responsibility during the acquisition process and responds quickly immediately following the acquisition.

- One aspect of HR management strategy for the target will be to make the employees of the target feel 'part of the family' under the new ownership. Consideration should be given to employee communication, including circulars and presentations, to social events and to team building initiatives.
- The requirements of the target in the new order may well involve redundancies and a refocusing of the target. It may be appropriate to adapt a wide ranging programme including retraining, redeployment, voluntary redundancy and early retirement.
- HR management is a continuing responsibility and it is likely that the purchaser will inherit some situations that are already in mid-sequence. For example, there may be disciplinary issues whereby an employee is already the subject of a warning and his performance is being monitored. It is important that the purchaser becomes involved in those issues immediately, for there is no concept of a period of grace in respect of such situations. Further, there could be a situation where, for example, an employee is under considerable stress. If that employee chose to leave and to bring an action for stress-related injury at work, the fact that there was a transfer of the business shortly before that employee left is unlikely to make any difference to the basis of the claim. It is important that the employer is able to identify such situations quickly and to deal with them. The most prudent course of action is to arrange an HR audit which would highlight such issues and allow them to be managed as a matter of priority. Ideally, this process of identifying such priority cases would begin well in advance of the transfer.
- The purchaser should be in a position in advance of the acquisition to make an assessment of the HR policies and procedures which are in place at the target and should be looking to fill any gaps and to improve policies and procedures as part of the post-acquisition review.
- If a target is being acquired by reason of the acquisition of shares, the personnel information will be the property of the target and should be immediately available to the purchaser. Where the acquisition includes a TUPE transfer, it will be necessary for the purchaser to have established a contractual right to the delivery of personnel files, for TUPE does not make provision for their transfer. It is important these are acquired as soon after completion as possible; indeed, ideally they

would be made available with effect from completion. The files would then be available for use in a prompt HR audit.

- The purchaser should consider what restrictive covenants may be appropriate in relation to the employees who have transferred under TUPE and the adequacy of those already in place should be reviewed in the context of the purchaser's group.

Notifying employees of a change of employer

Part I of the *Employment Rights Act 1996* sets out the rights of employees to a written statement of certain employment particulars. One item which must be contained in that statement is the name of the employer: see *Employment Rights Act 1996* section 1(3)(a).

Where the name of the employer changes, there is an obligation on the employer to inform the employee in writing of the change. This is likely to happen where there is a change in the identity of the employer consequent upon a transfer to which TUPE applies. It could, however, also arise in circumstances where there is a share transfer and where the name of the target company changes as a consequence of the transfer. Section 4 of the *Employment Rights Act 1996* requires that a statement containing particulars of the change must be given at the earliest opportunity and in any event not later than one month after the change in question. Provided that the legal identity of the employer does not change, or that where the identity of the employer changes there is no break in the continuity of employment, the statement may be limited to the name of the employer and need not restate the other terms and conditions of employment that would be required in a full statement under Part I of the *Employment Rights Act 1996*. Where there is a change in the identity of the employer but continuity is preserved, the statement of change must specify the date on which the employee's period of continuous service began (see section 4(8) *Employment Rights Act 1996*).

Given that this obligation could be fulfilled in one line of text, it is frequently satisfied by a note included with the pay slip or as part of an explanatory welcoming circular to employees. A precedent and drafting notes are to be found at page 111.

Chapter 7
Precedents (including drafting notes)

- Heads of Agreement
- Information requests
- Share and business sale/purchase agreements – key clauses
- Disclosure letters – key clauses
- Letters to employee representatives
- Section 4 Employment Rights Act 1996 Notices

Chapter 7
Precedents (including drafting notes)

Heads of Agreement

If Heads of Agreement are prepared in a transaction they are typically couched in general terms and it is unlikely that the parties will intend them to be legally binding, save in respect of issues such as confidentiality and lock-outs. By outlining the structure of the transaction which is proposed, a basis is established for subsequent negotiations and the preparation of definitive documentation. Although legal obligations may not be created, parties may find themselves subject to significant commercial pressure to follow the course mapped out in the Heads. It is important that employment considerations are given due consideration at this early stage, for the structure adopted is likely to dictate the employment law implications of the transaction.

Heads are unlikely to deal with employment issues in any details, if at all. A typical clause within Heads of Agreement relating to employment issues would be as follows:

> *'It shall be a working assumption that the Transfer of Undertakings (Protection of Employment) Regulations 2006 ('TUPE') apply to the sale of the Business. The definitive agreements shall contain indemnities in the usual form whereby all liabilities for the acts and omissions of the employer in respect of the period to Completion shall be the responsibility of the Vendor. The Purchaser shall assume responsibility for all employees of the Business following Completion. Any redundancy costs shall be borne by the Purchaser.'*

Information requests

It is appropriate for the purchaser to start from the assumption that, if he does not ask, he will not receive. The onus is on the purchaser to make such enquiries as he deems necessary in the course of taking a decision whether or not to make a purchase and the terms on which he is prepared to buy. At an early stage, therefore, it is usual for the purchaser to deliver an information request to the vendor in order to generate information concerning the target. Ordinarily, this is a checklist sent from the purchaser's solicitors to the vendor's solicitors, although the document itself will not normally have any legal effect.

A properly drafted sale/purchase agreement will exclude the possibility of the purchaser suing in reliance on any information generated by the exercise, for example by excluding the right to sue for misrepresentation, but the information generated by the request is likely in due course to form the core of the bundle of disclosure material and to drive the warranties and hence will take on a legal significance.

A common failing is for the purchaser's solicitors to adopt the 'kitchen sink' approach, delivering a standard form document drafted to cover a multitude of situations, without adequate editing. The danger of this approach is that inadequate attention is given to the key areas of the target and that the vendor's solicitors are confronted with a list of questions that are to a large extent meaningless. Nothing is more likely to encourage the vendor's solicitors to treat an information request with contempt than questions concerning Petroleum Revenue Tax asked in connection with the acquisition of a garden centre or the raising of enquiries concerning the handling of radioactive materials in connection with the acquisition of a bakery.

A far more effective way forward is to raise a request that is specifically tailored to the acquisition in prospect. This is likely to involve starting with a standard form but then deleting all those enquiries from the standard form that are manifestly not relevant and concentrating on drafting additional enquiries that relate to the specific concerns that arise in relation to the target. From an employment perspective, it is helpful if the purchaser's HR department and the employment specialist within the vendor's solicitors can address these concerns at the earliest stage. For example, a target may have had a particularly turbulent industrial relations history. It would be important to understand the reasons underlying these problems in order to predict whether it is likely that such problems will recur in future. Hence it may be appropriate to draft detailed questions about specific instances and to call for extensive disclosure of correspondence.

The precedent at page 78 relates to the employment aspects of the acquisition of a business. The form of this request would be modified in relation to the acquisition of shares, although not substantially. It forms part of a general information request. If a dialogue has already been established between the HR departments of the vendor and the purchaser and the employment lawyers advising the vendor and the purchaser, it may be appropriate for a dedicated employment information request to be prepared. If this course is taken, it is important that a careful record is made of all information disclosed, to ensure that in due course this information is taken into consideration when disclosures are being marshalled against the warranties in the sale/purchase agreement.

- The list is marked 'confidential'. Maintaining the status of the information as confidential is an important issue for the vendor: see further page 24 above. It is important that, when receiving the information disclosed under the request, the purchaser remains mindful of his obligations of confidentiality.
- The list is also marked 'subject to contract' – it is important that nothing is said in a document of this nature that evidences a contract having already been entered into. Marking the document in this express manner makes clear that any such inference that may have been raised is rebutted, that it is clear that the purchaser's intention to acquire the target has not yet become a legally binding obligation and that it is not intended that it should become so until definitive documents are agreed and signed.
- The starting point of the request must be a list of personnel engaged in work for the target **(question 1)**. Data protection laws will result in information being anonymised at this initial stage. Framing this request in relation to 'personnel employed by or engaged in the Business' allows the purchaser to see those working in the business of the target who are not employees. Special attention may need to be given to these workers, as they are unlikely to transfer to the employment of the purchaser by operation of law. The purchaser may have to enter into specific arrangements with any such workers in order to retain their services and it may be that the consent of a third party would be necessary, such as another company in the vendor's group or an independent contractor. **Question 5** is relevant in this context.
- Details such as age, sex and length of service allow the purchaser to see the profile of the target's personnel. These details will also be important in calculating the possible cost of declaring redundancies as a consequence of restructuring post-acquisition. Details of pay and notice periods are particularly relevant in this context, as are any policies specifically relevant to severance **(question 10)**. These may impose procedural obligations on the purchaser, such as selection criteria, and may make the cost of redundancy payments substantially greater than the statutory entitlements that would otherwise be payable.

- Questions concerning union membership can only be answered to the extent that the vendor is actually aware of this information. With the increase in direct debit arrangements between unions and their members and the consequent decline in check-off arrangements for collecting subscriptions, it is increasingly difficult to gather information to understand the profile of union membership within the target.
- Clearly, information is needed on the terms and conditions of employment of the employees of the target: hence **questions 2, 3 and 5**.
- A typical concern of the purchaser is to look ahead to how the target is to be integrated within the purchaser's group following the acquisition. Hence structural questions are likely to be relevant: see for example **question 6**. Bonus schemes, for example, will often have to be redesigned to fit the circumstances of the employment following the acquisition.
- **Question 7** is designed to obtain disclosure of employees whose existence would not be apparent from an inspection of the workplace. On the acquisition of shares, such employment relationships would persist unaffected. Moreover, in relation to the acquisition of a business to which TUPE applies, the fact that the transferee or the employee were unaware of the transfer is not material – see *Secretary of State for Industry v Cook* (supra).
- Compliance is always an issue: hence questions such as **16 and 17**. This provides a starting point until a full HR audit of the target can be conducted by the purchaser.
- **Question 21** is important: these costs can be expensive.

It is important to note that the information request is, ordinarily, merely the starting point. It will be appropriate to raise further requests consequent upon the disclosures or in relation to other concerns that become apparent in the course of the transaction.

CONFIDENTIAL
SUBJECT TO CONTRACT

Proposed acquisition by (the Purchaser) of the Business and the undertaking of (the Vendor)

Information Request

In connection with the proposed acquisition referred to above, the following information and copies of the following documents are requested. Please supply this information and the copy documents to [the offices of the Purchaser's solicitors] as soon as possible.

This list is not exhaustive and the Purchaser retains the right to request further information subsequently.

[Information requested under various headings – real estate; intellectual property; etc.]

EMPLOYMENT

1. A list of all personnel employed by or engaged in the Business with details of name, date of birth, sex, date of commencement of continuous employment, pay (including next review date) and other benefits, whether they are employed full-time or part-time (in which case, details of the extent of the employee's time commitment), notice periods, holiday entitlement, membership of pension scheme, normal retirement age, job title, location and (where known) details of union membership.
2. Standard terms and conditions of employment. Details of variations according to grade or job. Copy of staff handbook.
3. Details of all service agreements or terms of employment of directors and senior executives.
4. Details of any apprenticeship agreements, university/polytechnic student sponsorship agreements and any other scheme whereby any subsidy or allowance is paid to or in respect of any employee.
5. Details of any secondment agreements, consultancy agreements or any other agreement where employees are supplied by/to the Business.

6. Details of salary structure and progression. Details of any bonus or commission scheme. Details of any job evaluation/grading scheme in operation. Details of any pay review commitments and any pay negotiations currently in progress.

7. Details of employees on sick leave or maternity/paternity leave or other long term leave. Details of any sickness/disability schemes.

8. Details of all benefits provided to staff and to whom they are made available e.g. cars, medical benefits, membership of clubs, telephones.

9. Particulars of any recognised trade union; any applicable national or local trade union agreements; any staff association; the state of any current negotiations, dctails of grievance/disciplinary procedures and details of any labour disputes in the last three years. Details of any works council, staff council, elected body of employee representatives or similar. Details of all agreements entered into with any trade union or other body of employee representatives.

10. Details of any redundancy policy/severance scheme/early retirement programme.

11. Details of any current or threatened proceedings by former or current employees with further details of expected claims, if known. Brief details of any claims made by former or current employees during the past three years.

12. Details of any strikes or industrial action over the past three years.

13. Details of health and safety and equal opportunities policies.

14. Details of any Equality and Human Rights Commission (or any antecedent body)/HSE investigations/enquiries/recommendations over the past three years.

15. Details of each pension or life assurance scheme (approved or unapproved) operated by the Business or in which it participates (the 'schemes'), including...

16. Details of all "workers" within the Working Time Regulations not already included in the replies above. Details of all employees/workers who work more than 48 hours per week on average. Details of all employees/workers who are "night workers" within the Working Time Regulations. Copies of any individual, collective and workforce agreements entered into pursuant to the Working Time Regulations.
17. Details of all "workers" within the National Minimum Wage Regulations not already included in the replies above. Copies of any "fair estimate" agreements with employees/workers who perform output work pursuant to Regulation 25(1) of the National Minimum Wage Regulations. Copies of any "daily average" agreements with employees/workers who perform unmeasured work pursuant to Regulation 28(1) of the National Minimum Wage Regulations.
18. Details of all individuals in the undertaking working on training, work experience or similar schemes.
19. Details of all consultancy agreements or self-employed personnel.
20. Details of all employees who have notified the Vendor that they are pregnant or who are currently absent on maternity leave.
21. Details of all employees on long term sick leave together with confirmation of the nature of their illness.
22. Details of any share option scheme with confirmation of whether benefits under the scheme are discretionary or contractual and a copy of terms of the scheme.

Share and business sale/purchase agreements – key clauses

The employment lawyer and the HR manager will be concerned with certain aspects of these typically voluminous documents. The key areas are identified below on the contents page of a typical share sale/purchase agreement and a typical business sale/purchase agreement.

Share purchase agreement

Contents

1 Interpretation
2 Conditions
3 Sale and purchase of the shares
4 Consideration
5 Retention
6 Pre-completion matters
7 Completion
8 Warranties
9 Limitation on warranty and indemnity claims
10 Pensions
11 Confidentiality and announcements
12 Continuing obligations and assignment
13 Costs
14 Severability and suspension of restrictions
15 Entire agreement and variation
16 General provisions
17 Governing law and jurisdiction

Schedule I: The shares
Schedule II: The company and the subsidiaries
Schedule III: The properties
Schedule IV: The intellectual property rights
Schedule V: Warranties – general
Sechedule VI: Warranties – tax
Schedule VII: Pensions
Schedule VIII: Form of deed of covenant
Schedule IX: Form of tax deed of covenant

Business purchase agreement

Contents

The **interpretation clause**, ordinarily the first clause in the sale/purchase agreement, is the first item with which the employment lawyer and the HR manager need to be concerned.

It is of limited significance in the context of a share purchase agreement, but where a business is being acquired and TUPE applies, the clause is of considerable significance in the context of the definition of 'Employees'.

Under TUPE, those employees engaged in the business immediately prior to completion will transfer to the purchaser. The purchaser will want some certainty as to who he may expect to inherit. The definition is the cornerstone on which warranties and indemnities will be phrased to protect the purchaser against unforeseen liabilities. Hence the definition consists of two parts:

(a) The TUPE formula is repeated, in that 'Employees' are defined as 'the persons employed by the Vendor in the Business at the Completion Date; and

(b) Those whose names are set out in a schedule or appendix.

The clause should be drafted in such a way that, for a person to fall within the definition 'Employees', they must satisfy both of these two elements. Hence, an Employee for the purposes of the sale and purchase agreement is not merely an employee who would transfer under TUPE but an employee who would transfer under TUPE and whose name has been put on the agreed list.

The purchaser may therefore look at the agreed list of transferring employees in the knowledge that even if there are employees who transfer under TUPE, if they are not on the agreed list then although they will transfer by operation of law, the warranties and indemnities will protect him against liabilities that transfer with those employees.

This agreed list is at the centre of the whole issue of who transfers. Ordinarily, the issue of who transfers will never be raised before an employment tribunal. In the majority of cases, those employees who are on the agreed list of transferring employees will simply continue in the business and will be remunerated by the purchaser and no further thought will be given to the question. It is therefore the agreement between the vendor and the purchaser which is central to the question of which employees transfer. Equally, negotiation of the list is the key to which liabilities transfer.

In a share purchase, the purchaser will wish to ensure that he knows exactly who is employed by the target and on what terms. Again, this will be done by the disclosure of a list.

> *'Employees'* means the persons who are wholly or mainly employed by the Vendor in the Business at the Completion Date hereof whose names and details are set out in Schedule [ ].

The period between contract and completion must be the subject of specific agreement. Where the signature of the sale/purchase contract and completion of the transaction is not simultaneous, the purchaser will become under an obligation to buy the target but will not yet have assumed control, which will ordinarily not happen until completion. For a number of reasons, the purchaser will therefore wish to reach agreement with the vendor as to the basis on which the target will be run during this interim period, in particular so that the character of the target and its value is preserved.

In order to achieve this, a clause may be inserted, one aspect of which will be concerned with HR management during the interim period.

It is very much for the purchaser to decide what level of protection and involvement he needs. The clause on the following page is drafted on the basis that the target will continue to be managed in the ordinary course. It envisages no action on the part of the vendor to terminate or vary any terms of employment of any employee or to take on any new recruits without the prior written consent of the purchaser.

Alternative solutions would be to lay down certain criteria in accordance with which the vendor can manage the workforce without needing to consult the purchaser or to set up some sort of shadow management by the purchaser. Particular attention should be given to matters such as disciplinary procedures and material changes to terms and conditions. It may be impractical, for example, not to allow the vendor to continue to make HR decisions on a continuing basis.

If the purchaser is to take such a degree of control that TUPE will operate so as to transfer the employees in the business earlier than completion (see page 37 on this point), the sale/purchase agreement should be adjusted to reflect this – for example, warranties and indemnities should apply as from the date of transfer of the employers, not from completion.

Between the date hereof and Completion the Vendor will:

(a) Continue to carry on the Business in the ordinary and usual course so as to maintain the same as a going concern for its own benefit and at its own risk;

(b) Use all reasonable endeavours to protect the Goodwill for the benefit of the Purchaser and consult with the Purchaser with regard to the operation of the Business and cooperate with the Purchaser so as to ensure a smooth and efficient handover of the Business;

(c) Not to do or omit to do or cause or allow to be done or omitted to be done any act or thing which would result (or be likely to result) in a breach of any of the Warranties or which would or could jeopardise the Business or the Assets;

(d) Not enter into any material or significant transaction within the ordinary course of its business, nor into any contract or commitment of an unusual nature, nor institute any material change in its management policy;

(e) Maintain all subsisting policies of insurance relating to the Business and the Assets and shall forthwith obtain an endorsement of notice of the Purchaser's interest on the policy, the Vendor acknowledging that risk and property in the Assets shall pass to the Purchaser on Completion; and

(f) Not, without the prior written consent of the Purchaser, terminate or vary the remuneration or other terms of employment of any Employee, or enter into any new contract of employment.

Warranties provide protection against the unforeseen and will usually be provided in a detailed schedule. A clause (typically found somewhere in the middle of the sale and purchase agreement) will cross refer to the warranties and will explain their status, introducing qualifications and explaining the consequences of a breach.

Of particular concern are the clauses (clauses 5, 6 and 7 in the sample clause overleaf) whereby the scope of the warranties is restricted in terms of the financial implications of a breach. Typically, warranties will be limited on a de minimis basis, that is to say that unless an individual claim exceeds a certain threshold, a claim cannot be brought (the first part of clause 5 overleaf). Equally, unless the claims amount to a certain aggregate value, they may not be pursued against the vendor (the second part of clause 5 overleaf). The particular point to watch in the context of employment liabilities is that very often there may be a relatively small claim in respect of one employee, but if those claims are repeated over a large workforce, the aggregate value becomes considerable. Care should be taken that significant employment claims do not fall foul of this obstacle.

The overall value of the warranties will frequently be capped – for example by reference to the value of the consideration received by the vendor (see clause 6).

Indemnities are particularly attractive by reason of the fact that they speak directly to liabilities and are not subject to the same qualifications.

A time limit will ordinarily be imposed in respect of warranty claims (see clause 7 below). Claims brought under a contract of employment may be pursued subject to the ordinary limitation period for actions in contract which is six years from the date on which the course of action arose. In fact, employment liabilities are likely to be identified much earlier than that. Unfair dismissal claims must be brought within three months and it is in the nature of employment claims that they tend to become apparent in the short term.

Warranties

1 The Vendor hereby jointly and severally warrants to the Purchaser (save as set out in the Disclosure Letter) in the terms of the warranties set out in Schedule [ ] and undertakes with the Purchaser that each of the Warranties shall be true and accurate with effect from the Completion Date.

2 The Warranties shall be qualified by reference to those matters fully and fairly disclosed in the Disclosure Letter and not otherwise.

3 Each of the Warranties shall be construed as a separate and independent warranty, representation and undertaking and none of the Warranties shall be limited by reference to any other Warranty or by this Agreement.

4 The rights and remedies of the Purchaser in respect of any breach of warranty shall continue to subsist notwithstanding Completion.

5 No claim shall be made by the Purchaser for a breach of any of the Warranties unless the amount of any such claim exceeds [£] and unless the total amount of such claims when aggregated exceeds [£] but if such amount is exceeded the Vendor's liability shall be for the total amount of the said aggregate of claims and not merely the excess.

6 The liability of the Vendor in respect of the aggregate of all claims made by the Purchaser for breach of the Warranties shall not exceed the Consideration.

7 No claim may be brought by the Purchaser for breach of any of the Warranties unless written notice thereof shall have been given to the Vendor accompanied by reasonable details of the claim including the anticipated amount of the claim on or prior to the expiry of [ ] years as from the Completion Date.

8 Where any Warranty is qualified by an expression 'so far as the Vendor is aware' or any other similar expression, such expression shall be deemed to mean and include that the Vendor shall have made all due and careful enquiries.

9 Knowledge of any employee of the Vendor shall be deemed for the purposes of this Agreement to be knowledge of the Vendor.

10 The Vendor undertakes that, immediately upon becoming aware of any actual impending or threatened occurrence of any event after the date of this Agreement but before Completion which can reasonably be expected to cause or constitute a breach of any of the Warranties, it will forthwith give written notice to the Purchaser.

11 The Vendor agrees with the Purchaser (for itself and as trustee for the Employees) to assign to the Purchaser the rights, remedies or claims which it has or may have in respect of any misrepresentations in or omissions from any information or advice supplied or given by the Employees and on which they have relied in giving the Warranties, preparing the Disclosure Letter and for entering into this Agreement and/or the documents referred to herein.

The warranties themselves will be set out in some detail and it is the responsibility of the purchaser to ensure that warranties are taken in respect of each area of concern. There is really no such thing as a precedent set of warranties in that the warranties in each case must be tailored to the particular concerns raised by the circumstances of the transaction and the target business. To some extent, the warranties are likely to go hand in hand with the information request (see above). There will ordinarily be a separate section devoted to employment issues. The extract shows a typical set of warranties dealing with areas of central concern such as:

- Accurate details have been disclosed to the purchaser of all the employees falling within the definition of 'Employee' including details of terms and conditions and remuneration.
- A warranty to the effect that no one will transfer to the employment of the purchaser other than those falling within the definition of Employee.
- A warranty that no promises have been made in respect of salary increases.
- A warranty that none of the employees has given or received notice to terminate their employment.
- A warranty that there are no outstanding liabilities in respect of the employees.
- A warranty that there are no enhanced termination arrangements – this would be particularly significant if, for example, there was in place a contractual enhanced redundancy scheme resulting in enhanced payments being made to employees on redundancy. If the purchaser has it in mind to declare a number of redundancies, this could be considerably more expensive than might otherwise be envisaged.
- That there are no long term agreements with employees, in particular that there are no long term service contracts.
- Warranties concerning the position on union recognition and collective agreements.
- A warranty relating to equal opportunities measures in place and the target's track record on equal opportunities issues.
- A warranty relating to absent employees who may have a right to return, such as employees on long term sickness absence or maternity leave.
- A warranty as to potential litigation.
- A warranty relating to industrial action.

- A warranty that the vendor is not in breach of contract in relation to the employment contracts of the employees in the target.
- A warranty that full particulars of the terms and conditions of employment have been disclosed.
- A warranty that there is no disciplinary action current. This would be particularly useful in the context of putting the purchaser in a position to act quickly on any priority HR management issues.
- An explanation of the status of all non-employee workers within the target and the basis on which they are engaged.
- Confirmation that there are no loans outstanding to employees.
- Warranties that all information that ought to have been disclosed to employee representatives and all consultation that ought to have been carried out pursuant to Regulation 13 of TUPE has been undertaken. It should be noted in this context that any award made against a vendor for failure to inform and to consult under Regulation 13 of TUPE would be a concern to the Purchaser by reason of joint and several liability between transferor and transferee.
- A warranty relating to any insurance schemes.
- A 'sweeper' warranty relating to all contractual obligations between employer and employee.

It will be noted that some warranties are designed to generate the disclosure of information (for example 16) completely and accurately. Others are designed so as to provide protection against the unseen (for example 13). The vendor can comply with the first type of warranty by making full disclosure of the information which is the subject of the warranty. As for the second type of warranty, the vendor may qualify the warranty by listing exceptions in the disclosure letter. For example, if warranty 13 could be given subject to the fact that there is one employee on maternity leave, then that exception should be listed in the disclosure letter, which qualifies the warranties.

Warranties – Employees

1 The particulars shown in the Disclosure Letter provide the names of each Employee and accurate details of their terms and conditions of employment including, without limitation, all remuneration and other benefits, whether contractual or otherwise, payable now or at any time hereafter to each of the Employees or any person connected with any Employee as well as particulars of all profit sharing incentive and bonus arrangements to which the Vendor is a party or which are applicable to any of the Employees whether legally binding on the Vendor or not. There is no contractual or other obligation (including any established practice) to increase or otherwise vary any such remuneration or benefits of any Employee. No person is employed or engaged in the Business (whether under a contract of employment or a contract for services) other than the Employees and those persons referred to in the Disclosure Letter and the Vendor has not offered any contract of employment or contract for services to any other person. The Employees are all employed by the Vendor (and not jointly with any other employer) and each Employee is employed exclusively in the Business.

2 All the Employees work full-time in the Business.

3 None of the Employees have given or received notice terminating his employment nor is there any liability outstanding to such persons except for remuneration or other benefits accruing due and all such remuneration or other benefit which has fallen due for payment has been paid. So far as the Vendor is aware, no Employee objects to the transfer of their employment to the Purchaser for the purpose of Regulation 4(7) of the Regulations.

4 No Employee will be entitled as a result of or in connection with this Agreement:

   1 to terminate his employment with the Vendor;

   2 to receive any payment, reward or benefit of any kind;

   3 to receive any enhancement in or improvement to his remuneration, benefits or terms and conditions of employment; or

   4 to treat himself as being dismissed on the ground of redundancy or otherwise released from any obligation to the Vendor.

5 The aggregate level of remuneration payable to Employees has not increased by more than [3] per cent within the last 12 months.

6 It is not the common practice of the Vendor to increase remuneration payable to any Employee on an annual basis and there is no contractual or other obligation to increase or otherwise vary the remuneration payable to any Employee.

The Vendor has not within the last [12] months:

1 increased or offered or agreed to increase the remuneration of, or

2 altered or offered or sought to alter any of the terms and conditions of employment of any Employee, nor are any negotiations for any such increase or alterations expected or likely to take place within the next 6 months.

7 There is no plan scheme commitment or established practice relating to the termination of employment affecting any of the Employees more generous than the statutory redundancy entitlement or such sum as may properly be payable by way of bona fide damages for breach of contract.

8 There are no subsisting agreements between the Vendor and any Employee which are not terminable by the Vendor without compensation (other than any compensation payable by statute) on three months notice or less given at any time.

9 The Vendor has not recognised any trade union or other body representing any of the Employees nor entered into any agreement arrangement or negotiation with any trade union. There are no collective agreements in force with any trade union or similar organisation. There is no works council established in respect of the Business.

10 There are no enquiries or investigations existing, pending or threatened in relation to the Business by the Equal Opportunities Commission, the Commission for Racial Equality, the Disability Rights Commission or any similar authority, neither have there been any such enquiries or investigations in the period of three years ending on the Completion Date.

11 There is no liability, outstanding or contingent or anticipated, to any present or former Employee other than remuneration accrued for the current wage or salary period or for reimbursement of normal business expenses.

No present or former Employee or any applicant for any role in the Business has any:

1 claim, outstanding or contingent or anticipated, against or

2 right to be indemnified by the Vendor arising out of an act or omission by the Vendor on or before the date of this Agreement and [so far as the Vendor is aware] there are [no] facts or circumstances that might give rise to the same.

12 None of the Employees has at the date of this Agreement any:

1 accrued rights to holiday pay or to pay in lieu of holidays [which have not been provided for in full in the Management Accounts];

2 loan or advance or has received any financial assistance from the Vendor;

3 outstanding claim under any PHI or medical expenses insurance scheme provided by the Vendor;

4 right, now or in the future:

(a) to return to work (whether for reasons connected with maternity, paternity, adoption or parental leave or absence by reason of illness or incapacity, secondment or otherwise);

(b) to be reinstated or re-engaged by the Vendor; or

(c) to any other compensation.

13 None of the Employees or other persons previously working in the Business who have or may have a statutory or contractual right to return to work in the Business are on maternity leave, absent on grounds of disability or other leave of absence.

14 The Vendor is not aware of any acts or omission, the result of which is reasonably likely to result in litigation against the Purchaser by any of the Employees. No industrial action is being taken or is likely to be taken or has been threatened by any of

the Employees or any trade union against the Vendor or any Vendor Group company in relation to the Business, nor has any such action been taken or threatened in the last three years, and during the six months preceding the date of this Agreement there has been no material adverse change in relations between the Vendor and the Employees. There is no current dispute with all or any of the Employees that is reasonably likely to result in litigation or any form of collective action. There is no current notice of industrial action pursuant to Section 234A of the Trade Union and Labour Relations Act 1992.

15 The Vendor is not in breach of the contract of employment of any of the Employees and has complied in all respects with all obligations imposed on it by all statutes, regulations and codes of conduct and practices relevant to the relations between it and the Employees.

16 A full copy of the standard terms of employment of the Employees (including, without limitation, any staff handbook) and an up-to-date copy of the terms of employment of each Employee employed on terms other than the standard terms is attached to the Disclosure Letter.

17 None of the Employees is subject to any disciplinary action or engaged in any grievance procedure and there is no matter or fact which can be reasonably foreseen as likely to give rise to the same.

18 The terms on which all consultants and other independent contractors are engaged in the Business are described in or attached to the Disclosure Letter together with an exhaustive list of all such persons. HM Revenue and Customs have confirmed in writing that it does not consider any such person to be an employee of the Vendor or any Vendor Group company.

19 There are no loans outstanding from the Vendor or any Vendor Group company to any of the Employees.

20 The Vendor has complied with all obligations to inform and consult pursuant to Regulation 13.

21 None of the Employees are receiving or are due to receive payments under any disability or permanent health or any similar

insurance scheme and there are no claims pending or threatened or any circumstances which may give rise to such a claim by any of the Employees against the Vendor in respect of any accident, injury, debility or ill-health. No employee is suffering from or has suffered in the last 12 months from any medical or other condition which impairs or might impair his or her ability to continue to perform their duties and/or which requires or might require any arrangement or adjustment within the workplace.

22 The Vendor has performed all material obligations and duties required to be performed by it whether arising under contract, statute, at common law or otherwise in respect of each of the Employees. There are no amounts outstanding or promised to any of the Employees and no liability has been incurred by the Vendor which remains undischarged for breach of any contract of service or for redundancy payments, statutory or otherwise, (including protective awards) or for compensation or any awards under any employment legislation or regulation or for wrongful dismissal or unfair dismissal or otherwise and no order has been made at any time for the reinstatement or re-engagement of any of the Employees or any person formerly employed or engaged in the Business.

23 No Employee has made a protected disclosure for the purposes of the Employment Rights Act 1996 at any time during the last 12 months.

24 The Vendor has, in relation to each of the Employees:

1.35.1 complied and continues to comply [in all material respects] with all obligations, awards, orders and recommendations imposed on it or made by or under statute, statutory instrument, European Union law, common law, contract, any collective agreement, the terms and conditions of employment, staff handbook, company policy, any customs and practice and any codes of conduct and practice;

1.35.2 complied and continues to comply with any recommendations made by the Advisory Conciliation and Arbitration Service, the Equality and Human Rights Commission the Central Arbitration Committee or any other bodies with similar functions or powers in relation to employees, and with any arbitration awards and declarations; and

1.35.3 maintained and continues to maintain adequate and suitable personnel records (including records of working time) which are up to date, complete and accurate.

25 All Employees have leave to enter and remain in the United Kingdom and are entitled to work in the United Kingdom under the Asylum and Immigration Act 1996.

In a share sale/purchase agreement it is unlikely that there would be a clause dealing specifically with employees. This is principally because the relationship between employer and employee is unchanged by reason of the transfer of shares.

In an asset sale and purchase agreement, it is likely that there will be a specific section of the agreement dealing with employees, such as that reproduced below. The purpose of this section is to set out the assumptions of the parties as to whether or not TUPE applies and to provide for a readjustment in circumstances where that assumption is not borne out by a subsequent decision of an employment tribunal.

In the sample text, the first part of clause 1 records the assumption on which the parties are entering into the transaction. It is assumed that TUPE will apply and the clause commits both parties to acting on that basis.

Both parties need to consider what the position would be if TUPE was held not to apply. For example, if the employees are crucial to the purchaser, the purchaser may wish to oblige the vendor in such circumstances to make the employees available on a consultancy basis if they do not transfer by operation of law. Equally, the vendor would be left with employees and the potential for liabilities such as dismissal costs – the vendor would want to oblige the purchaser to make offers of employment to the employees in such circumstances.

Clauses 4 and 5 are indemnities in relation to the matters set out in the sub-sections of the clause. It is often very difficult to obtain assurance on an indemnity basis within a sale and purchase agreement, but employment liabilities of this nature are one area in which an indemnity is both appropriate and frequently obtained.

A key component of the indemnity in favour of the purchaser is in clause 5.1, providing that if anyone who is not in the agreed list of Employees brings a claim against the purchaser alleging that he has transferred under TUPE and that obligations he had against the vendor have become obligations of the purchaser, those liabilities must be reimbursed to the purchaser by the vendor.

The other key aspect of the indemnity in favour of the purchaser is in respect of any act or omission of the vendor prior to completion. These liabilities will transfer under TUPE and yet will have arisen during a period when the purchaser will have had no responsibility for the running of the business.

The indemnity in favour of the vendor is necessary to ensure that the purchaser accepts full responsibility for the period post-completion; also for any acts and omissions of the purchaser prior to completion which give rise to a liability for the vendor.

For sake of clarity, clauses 8 and 9 make it plain that the obligation of the vendor is to pay all employment-related liabilities up to completion and that the purchaser shall assume responsibility for such payments following completion. Equally, clauses of this nature could come in a general section of the sale/purchase agreement devoted to apportionments. The sums at issue in respect of a transaction completed in the middle of a payroll month could be quite significant. Without a clause of this nature, the purchaser would be liable for all arrears and the vendor would not receive any credit for any pre-payments.

Transfer of Employees

1 The Vendor and Purchaser intend and acknowledge that the transfer of the Business to the Purchaser on Completion shall, with respect to the Employees, constitute a Relevant Transfer, and agree that as a consequence of that Relevant Transfer, the contracts of employment made between the Vendor and the Employees (save insofar as such contracts relate to benefits for old age, invalidity or survivors under any occupational pension scheme) will have effect from and after Completion as if originally made between the Purchaser and the Employees.

2 Notwithstanding the acknowledgement and agreement in Clause 1 above, and in recognition of the possibility that the transfer of the Business may be determined not to be a Relevant Transfer by a court or tribunal, the Purchaser shall, with effect

from Completion, offer employment to each Employee on like terms to the terms on which they would have become employed by the Purchaser had there been a Relevant Transfer, or, to the extent that it is not reasonably practicable to do so in respect of any such term, on terms which are not in such respect materially to the detriment of the Employee.

3 The Purchaser shall treat the period of continuous service of each Employee with the Vendor up to Completion as continuous with such Employee's service with the Buyer.

Indemnities

4 The Vendor shall indemnify the Purchaser against all costs, claims, liabilities and expenses (including legal expenses on an indemnity basis) incurred in connection with or as a result of:

4.1 any claim or demand by any Employee (whether in tort, contract, under statute, pursuant to European law or otherwise including, without limitation, any claim for unfair dismissal, wrongful dismissal, a redundancy payment, breach of contract, unlawful deduction from wages, discrimination on the grounds of sex, race, disability, age, sexual orientation, religion or religious belief, a protective award or a claim or demand of any other nature in each case arising directly or indirectly from any act, fault or omission (or any alleged act, fault or omission) of the Vendor in respect of any Employee prior to Completion;

4.2 any claim or demand by any person (other than an Employee) that their employment or any liability relating thereto has or should have transferred to the Purchaser by reason of their Agreement;

4.3 any failure by the Vendor to comply with its obligations under regulation 13 of the Regulations; and

4.4 any claim (including any individual employee entitlement under or consequent on such claim) by any trade union or other body or person representing the Employees arising from or connected with the failure by the Vendor to comply with any legal obligation to such trade union, body or person.

5 The Purchaser shall indemnify the Vendor against all costs, claims, liabilities and expenses (including legal expenses on an indemnity basis) incurred in connection with or as a result of:

5.1 any claim or demand by any Employee (whether in contract, tort, under statute, pursuant to European law or otherwise) including, without limitation, any claim for unfair dismissal, wrongful dismissal, a redundancy payment, breach of contract, unlawful deduction from wages, discrimination on the grounds of sex, race, disability, age, sexual orientation, religion or religious belief, a protective award or a claim or demand of any other nature in each case arising directly or indirectly from any act, fault or omission (or any alleged act, fault or omission) of the Purchaser in respect of any Employee and whether arising before, on or after Completion;

5.2 any failure by the Purchaser to comply with its obligations under Regulation 13 of the Regulations;

5.3 any claim (including any individual employee entitlement under or consequent on such claim) by any trade union or other body or person representing the Employees arising from or connected with any failure by the Purchaser to comply with any legal obligation to such trade union, body or person whether any such claim arises before, on or after Completion;

5.4 any change or proposed change in the terms and conditions of employment or working conditions of the Employees on or after their transfer to the Purchaser on Completion, or to the terms and conditions of employment or working conditions of any person who would have been an Employee but for their resignation (or decision to treat their employment as terminated under Regulation 4(9) of the Regulations) on or before Completion as a result of any such proposed changes;

5.5 the change of identity of employer occurring by virtue of the Regulations and/or this Agreement being significant and detrimental to any of the Employees, or to any person who would have been an Employee but for their resignation (or decision to treat their employment as terminated under Regulation 4(9) of the Regulations) on or before Completion as a result of the change in employer;

6 If it is found or alleged that any of the Employees remains an employee of the Vendor after Completion:

6.1 the Vendor shall notify the Purchaser of that finding or allegation as soon as reasonably practicable after becoming aware of it;

6.2 in consultation with the Vendor, the Purchaser shall within [7] days of becoming aware of the finding or allegation make that person a written offer of employment to commence immediately on the same terms and conditions as thc Purchaser would be obliged to provide to that person if his employment had transferred pursuant to the Regulations and under which the Purchaser agrees to recognise that person's period of service with the Vendor;

6.3 If the offer of employment made by the Purchaser is accepted by that person, the Vendor agrees to permit that person to leave the Vendor's employment without having worked his full notice period, if that person so requests;

6.4 Upon the offer being made as referred to in Clause 6.2 (or at any time after the expiry of the [7] days if the offer is not made as requested), the Purchaser may dismiss that person with immediate effect; and

6.5 the Purchaser shall indemnify the Vendor against all costs, claims, liabilities and expenses (including legal expenses on an indemnity basis) which the Vendor may suffer or incur in respect of that dismissal.

7 Where the Vendor is entitled to an indemnity from the Purchaser pursuant to this clause [1], the Vendor may in its absolute discretion defend, settle or compromise any claim referred to within the said indemnity and the Purchaser will on demand indemnify the Vendor against all costs, claims, liabilities and expenses (including legal expenses on an indemnity basis) arising out of, or in connection with, the Vendor so doing.

8 The Vendor shall be responsible for all emoluments and outgoings in respect of the Employees (including without limitation all wages, bonuses, commissions, PAYE, national insurance contributions and pension contributions) which are attributable to the period up to and including Completion.

9 The Purchaser shall be responsible for all emoluments and outgoings in respect of the Employees (including without limitation all wages, bonuses, commissions, PAYE, national insurance contributions and pension contributions) which are attributable to the period after Completion (including any bonuses or commission which are payable before Completion but which are attributable to the period after Completion), and will indemnify the Vendor against all costs, claims, liabilities and expenses (including reasonable legal expenses) in respect of the same.

10 The Purchaser will assume the outstanding obligations of the Vendor in respect of any accrued holiday entitlements and accrued holiday remuneration of the Employees at Completion.

Set out below is a clause for use where the transaction does not, in the view of the parties, constitute a TUPE transfer or where it is not the intention of the parties that the employees will transfer. This will be a relatively rare occurrence.

EITHER

1 The Vendor and the Purchaser believe that the sale of the Business does not amount to the transfer of an undertaking for the purposes of the Regulations and/or the Directive and no person employed in the Business will be employed by the Purchaser following the transfer of the Business.

OR

1 It is not the intention of the parties that any past or present employees of the Vendor will be employed by the Purchaser following the transfer of the Business.

2 If as a result of the sale of the Business and/or the application of the Regulations and/or the Directive, any past or present employee of the Vendor shall become, or otherwise be deemed to be, or shall claim or is alleged to have become, an employee of the Purchaser:

2.1 the Purchaser shall notify the Vendor of that fact or allegation as soon as reasonably practicable after becoming aware of it;

2.2 in consultation with the Purchaser, the Vendor shall within [7] days of becoming aware of that fact or allegation make that person a written offer of employment to commence immediately on the same terms and conditions as that person was employed immediately prior to the transfer (actual or alleged), and under which the Vendor agrees to recognise that person's prior service with the Vendor;

2.3 upon the offer being made as referred to in Clause 2.2 (or at any time after the expiry of the [7] days if the offer is not made as requested), the Purchaser may dismiss that person concerned with immediate effect;

2.4 the Vendor shall indemnify the Purchaser against all costs, claims, liabilities and expenses (including legal expenses on an indemnity basis) in connection with or as a result of:

(a) any claim or demand by that person (whether in contract, tort, under statute, pursuant to European law or otherwise) including, without limitation, any claim for unfair dismissal, wrongful dismissal, a redundancy payment, breach of contract, unlawful deduction from wages, discrimination on the grounds of sex, race or disability, sexual orientation, religion or religious belief, a protective award or a claim or demand of any other nature and whether arising before, on or after Completion;

(b) any failure by the Vendor to comply with its obligations under Regulations 13 and 14 of the Regulations, or any award of compensation under Regulation 15 of the Regulations;

(c) any claim (including any individual employee entitlement under or consequent on such a claim) by any trade union or other body or person arising from or connected with any failure by the Vendor to comply with any legal obligation to such trade union, body or person whether any such claim arises before, on or after Completion.

3 Where the Purchaser is entitled to an indemnity from the Vendor pursuant to this clause, the Purchaser may in its absolute discretion defend, settle or compromise any claim referred to within the said indemnity and the Vendor will on demand indemnify the Purchaser against all costs, claims, liabilities and expenses (including legal expenses on an indemnity basis) arising out of, or in connection with the Purchaser so doing.

Disclosure letters – key clauses

The disclosure letter is a document which is delivered by the vendor or the vendor's solicitors to the purchaser or the purchaser's solicitors and qualifies the warranties given in the sale and purchase agreement. In essence, it seeks to put the purchaser on notice of certain information and to preclude the purchaser from relying on such information in pursuing a warranty claim.

Typically, these disclosure letters are drafted in two sections. The first section, which is capable of being the subject of a precedent such as that reproduced below, deals with the 'disclosure' of certain general information, whereby it is agreed that certain information is deemed to be within the knowledge of the purchaser, for example information which is in the public domain, information which may be found in certain sources such as the vendor's annual report and accounts or information held at the Land Registry.

A disclosure bundle will be made up from information which has been generated by the target and supplied to the purchaser and will form an appendix to the disclosure letter. That information, which will form an agreed bundle, is deemed to be within the knowledge of the purchaser and qualifies the warranties in respect of any breach of warranty claim. A set of specific disclosures will then disclose information by reference to specific warranties.

The way in which this works may be illustrated by turning back to the warranties reproduced above on page 87. Warranty 7 is seeking to establish that there are no enhanced severance schemes whereby employees may be entitled to a larger payment than the statutory minimum. Let us assume that there are, in fact, two enhanced schemes in place – a group severance policy which applies to all employees, providing a redundancy payment greater than the statutory minimum; and a letter of assurance has also been given to a senior executive that in the event of the target being sold within a certain time scale, he will receive an enhanced redundancy payment.

The vendor should disclose those two schemes against the warranty. Once disclosed, by a specific disclosure cross-referring to the warranty, the purchaser has knowledge of those schemes. The appropriate course of action for the purchaser in these circumstances is to seek an adjustment in the purchase price. For example, the purchaser may have assumed a certain level of redundancy costs in his projections relating to the acquisition. If those costs are now thrown out by the existence of the enhanced redundancy scheme, he should seek a reduction in the purchase price to take into account the increased costs that he will have to bear.

If, by oversight or lack of communication between the vendor and its advisers, a scheme is not disclosed, for example the agreement with the senior executive has not come to the attention of the vendor's lawyers and is not included in the disclosure letter, and it only comes to the notice of the purchaser following the acquisition, then the purchaser will be entitled to rely on the warranty and will have a claim against the vendor for any additional liability arising by reason of the enhanced scheme agreed with the senior executive.

Draft Disclosure Letter

[Letterhead of Vendor's Solicitors]

TO: [insert details of solicitors acting for the purchaser]

DATED: [ ]

Dear Sirs

RE: [ ] LIMITED (THE 'COMPANY')

This letter together with all the documents attached to or referred to in it (the 'Disclosure Bundle') is the Disclosure Letter referred to in Clause [ ] and defined in Clause [ ] of an agreement of even date herewith entered into between [ ], [ ] and [ ] relating to the sale and purchase of the whole of the issued share capital in the Company (the 'Agreement').

The definitions in the Agreement shall (unless the context otherwise requires) apply to this Disclosure Letter.

If there are any inconsistencies between the provisions and contents of this Disclosure Letter and the Agreement, this Disclosure Letter and the Schedules hereto shall prevail and shall be deemed to be the relevant disclosure.

The provisions and contents of the documents attached to this Disclosure Letter shall, in the event of any inconsistency, prevail over the summaries of those documents contained in this Disclosure Letter.

The Purchaser's solicitors have been notified of the existence of the documents listed or referred to in the Schedule hereto and the contents of all such documents shall be deemed to have been disclosed to the Purchaser prior to the date of the Agreement whether or not such documents (or copies thereof) have been delivered to the Purchaser or its solicitors. Accordingly, the Vendor shall not be and shall not be deemed to be in breach of any of the representations, warranties and undertakings set out in the Agreement insofar as such representation, warranty or undertaking touches or concerns any matter or document or any other information contained or referred to in this Disclosure Letter or the Schedule hereto.

Where a document is referred to herein as being disclosed but is not attached, all information contained in that document is deemed to be herein disclosed. Where brief particulars only of the matter are set out or referred to in this Disclosure Letter it is assumed that the Purchaser does not require further details of such matters.

This Disclosure Letter has been prepared by this firm from information made available to it by or on behalf of the Vendor. In no event is any liability to any person accepted by this firm for the accuracy or otherwise of the information contained herein.

The disclosures herein and in the Schedule hereto are made on the basis that each matter disclosed in relation to a particular warranty is effective generally in relation to each and every warranty as may be appropriate, and each such disclosure is given without prejudice to the generality and effectiveness of any other disclosure. Without prejudice to the foregoing, for the sake of convenience only certain disclosures under the heading 'Specific Disclosures' are recorded against particular warranties.

The representations, warranties and undertakings in the Agreement shall not apply to any matter, fact or event which is attributable to or appeared in the period preceding the date on which the Vendor acquired the Company.

GENERAL DISCLOSURES

This Disclosure Letter shall be deemed to include and there are hereby incorporated into it by reference as having been generally disclosed the following matters:

1. The contents of and all the information contained in or ascertainable from the documents attached to this Disclosure Letter or referred to in the Schedule.

2. Any information contained or referred to on the files maintained by the Registrar of Companies in England and Wales on the business day immediately preceding the date hereof in respect of the Company.

3. Any matter or information referred to or contained in any statutory books and registers of the Company which has been produced for inspection by or on behalf of the Purchaser prior

to the date hereof, including without limitation, the Memorandum and Articles of Association of the Company.

4. Any matter or transaction to the extent that the same is disclosed in the Agreement.

5. The Accounts of the Company together with the reports and statements attached thereto and all the notes attached to any of the Accounts.

6. All matters contained in all correspondence up to and including the date hereof passing from the Company, the Vendor, their solicitors or accountants, actuaries, surveyors and other advisers and agents to the Purchaser or its solicitors, accountants, actuaries, surveyors and other advisers and agents together with all enclosures attached to or enclosed therewith and all matters referred to in such enclosures.

7. All information in the public domain.

[Various addition general disclosures not relating to employment issues.]

SPECIFIC DISCLOSURES

Without prejudice to the generality of the foregoing we disclose the matters set out below which, for ease of reference only, appear against the paragraph numbers in Schedule [ ] of the Agreement to which they most obviously relate but each paragraph below shall be deemed to have been disclosed in relation to every representation, warranty and undertaking in the Agreement:

[Insert Specific Disclosures: e.g.:

7. The Vendor's group severance policy applies to all employees of the Company. A copy of this policy is attached to this letter.

9. The Company has entered into a recognition agreement with the TGWU in relation to hourly paid workers at the [ ] factory. A copy of that agreement is attached to this letter.

17. A Mr AB Smith is under a final written warning following persistent absenteeism.]

Please acknowledge receipt of this letter by signing the acknowledgement on the enclosed duplicate and returning it to us; such signature and return will constitute your confirmation that the disclosures in this letter are accepted for the purposes of the Agreement on the basis stated in this Disclosure Letter.

Yours faithfully

[Vendor's solicitors]

We acknowledge receipt of the Disclosure Letter of which this is a copy and of each of the documents referred in the Schedule thereto. We confirm on behalf of our client that the Disclosure Letter and all things contained therein are disclosed in accordance with the terms of the Disclosure Letter.

....

Dated [ ] day of [ ] 199[ ]

Letters to employee representatives

The obligations on a vendor to disclose information to employee representatives pursuant to Regulation 13 of TUPE is explained above at page 57. Overleaf is a sample letter setting out such information. In fact, the letter does little more than set out the bare information required to be disclosed under Regulation 13(2) of TUPE, following the text of Regulation 13(2) itself.

In the context of an information and disclosure exercise, it may well be that substantially more information will be disclosed. However, a letter of this nature is often the appropriate formal step to comply with the core obligation and to set the information and consultation exercise in motion.

Dear Sirs

Proposed disposal of the [ ] division of [ ] Limited to [ ] Limited

The purpose of this letter is to advise you that we propose to sell our [ ] division to [ ] Limited. In advance of this proposed sale, this letter contains information which we are obliged to deliver to you under Regulation 13(2) of the Transfer of Undertakings (Protection of Employment) Regulations 2006 ('TUPE').

(a) We are intending that the sale will be completed on or about [ ];

(b) The reason for the transfer is the fact that the Company is seeking to channel its resources into its core businesses. The [ ] division is not seen as part of the Company's core businesses and requires funds that are not available to it within the Company in order to invest and expand its product range;

(c) The legal implications of the transfer are that it is anticipated that TUPE will apply to transfer the employment of the division's employees (on the basis of current terms and conditions and with a preservation of statutory continuity) to [ ] Limited;

(d) It is not envisaged that there will be any economic or social implications of the transfer for employees save that membership of the Company's pension scheme will cease with effect from the transfer;

(e) We are informed that [ ] does not intend to take any measures in connection with the transfer in relation to any of the affected employees.

As neither we nor [ ] envisage that any measures will be taken in relation to the transfer, no consultation is required under TUPE. If that position changes we shall let you know with a view to entering into consultations in relation to the same.

Please do not hesitate to contact me if you have any queries.

Yours faithfully

Where redundancies are proposed, obligations may be triggered under section 188 of the Trade Union and Labour Relations (Consolidation) Act 1992 (see page 62 above). There are obligations to give a certain amount of notice for consultation purposes and to disclose certain information in relation to the proposals. The letter set out below is a suggested formal letter in response to the statutory requirements of section 188. In practice, it is likely that much more extensive disclosure will be made as discussions get under way.

Dear Sirs

Proposed redundancies within the [ ] division of [ ] Limited.

Following the acquisition of the [ ] division from [ ] Limited it has become clear to us that, to ensure the continuing viability of this business, certain cost-savings will need to be implemented. One aspect of this will be to address over-manning within the division.

It is proposed that a number of redundancies will be declared. It is proposed that out of the 100 works staff, 20 individuals will be made redundant. Of these, 10 will be skilled labour and 10 will be unskilled labour. Out of the 150 staff employees, it is proposed to make redundant 15 employees of whom 10 are secretarial/clerical and five managerial.

The proposed method of selection of employees is in accordance with the collective agreement between [union] and [ ] Limited dated [ ], that is to say an evaluation of each employee scored by reference to the following factors:

(1) Consideration of the balance of skills within the workforce and the future needs of the division;

(2) Performance, ability and time-keeping;

(3) Length of service.

It is proposed that after a period of consultation between us of 30 days from the date of this letter, the first dismissal will take effect. It is proposed that selected employees will work for two weeks of their notice period (which will run from the expiry of our 30-day consultation period) and will then leave with the balance of any notice monies due to them being discharged with a payment in lieu of notice.

I am enclosing a copy of Form HR1 sent to the Secretary of State under section 193 of the Trade Union and Labour Relations (Consolidation) Act 1992. I am also informing you that today I am posting a notice regarding the above proposals on works notice boards.

I look forward to hearing from you with any representations you may wish to make upon the above proposals in order that consultation can now begin.

Yours faithfully

Section 4 Employment Rights Act 1996 Notices

Where TUPE applies to the transfer of a business, contracts of employment will transfer by operation of law as described above. As a matter of contract law, therefore, there is no need to issue any further documentation or to reach any supplemental agreement. There may, however, be a need to issue further documentation for two reasons:

- As a matter of good HR management practice, to record the details of the employment contract post-acquisition.
- To comply with Part I of the Employment Rights Act 1996.

Although the contract of employment transfers automatically by reason of TUPE, there will doubtless be changes. The identity of the employer will have changed; occupational pension scheme rights will not have transferred and new pension arrangements may be in place; there may be certain other rights specifically related to the vendor such as share option rights which have not transferred. Equally it may be that the purchaser will wish to offer certain other benefits. As a matter of good HR management practice it is advisable to ensure that the contractual rights and obligations of the transferred employees are clear.

Moreover, the purchaser should ensure that the obligations arising under Section 1 of the Employment Rights Act 1996 have been complied with – namely the obligation to give an employee a written statement of certain basic terms and conditions of employment. Even if that obligation has been complied with, there will have been changes, if only a change in the identity of the employer. Under

Section 4 of the Employment Rights Act 1996, there is an obligation on employers to advise employees in writing of any changes to any of the items required to be included in the written statement. The notification must be made at the earliest opportunity and in any event within one month of the change.

There is no particular prescribed form for the statement and it may be that the changes could be included in another document, such as a letter of welcome. If the intention is to issue a supplemental statement merely to comply with the basic legal obligation under Section 4, the following could be used. Typically such a statement may be issued by including it with the next pay slip.

Where there has been a transfer of shares, the employment contract will not ordinarily have been affected, but it may be that there have been changes, for example because the employees are unable to continue to participate in the vendor's group pension scheme. Any such changes should be recorded in writing as a matter of good HR management practice and a written statement under Section 4 of the Employment Rights Act 1996 may also be required.

Statement of changes to the written statement of terms and conditions of employment

(Issued pursuant to Section 4, Employment Rights Act 1996)

[Date]

With effect from [date of transfer] your employer became [name] of [address].

Your period of continuous employment began on [ ].

[All other terms and conditions of employment remain unaffected.] [Refer to any other changes.]

Other specially commissioned briefings from Thorogood

BUSINESS AND COMMERCIAL LAW

Commercial Contracts: Legal principles and drafting

Burnett, Rachel • £145 ISBN: 978-185418702-4

This briefing takes into account relevant legislation and case law. For all points of the law and critical distinctions, you will find crystal-clear explanations and guidelines to a host of case studies illustrating the law and its application.

Commercial Litigation: Damages and other remedies for breach of contract

Ribeiro, Robert • £145 ISBN: 978-185418397-2

A great deal has changed in the last few years... a new emphasis on claims for damages such as loss of business, opportunity, chance, use and data and recent landmark cases have altered the ground-rules. Completely updated, this briefing includes accounts of all the most recent important cases and highlights significant changes in the way that the courts now assess damages.

Corporate Governance

Martin, David • £99 ISBN: 978-185418354-5

This briefing is a clear, accessible and jargon-free analysis of the practical application of Corporate Governance. With short case studies to illustrate legal requirements, the author guides the reader through all aspects of the Corporate Governance programme, concentrating specifically on its use by organisations who are not required to adopt it, such as listed PLCs.

Email: Legal issues 2008

Singleton, Susan • £125 ISBN: 978-185418630-0

One of the biggest changes to office life in the last five years has been the growth of e-mail. On balance a major advantage to businesses, enabling postage charges and time to be saved, but e-mail also comes with certain legal risks.

This report seeks to highlight those areas where employers particularly need to consider relevant risks. However in most cases the risks can be minimised to an acceptable level and nothing with this report should put any employer off letting their employees loose on e-mail. It highlights principal issues which arise and the means to ensure enforcement, in particular, by presenting to employees a coherent e-mail and Internet use policy so they know where they stand.

For full details of any title, and to view sample extracts, please visit:
www.thorogoodpublishing.co.uk

Freedom of Information Act in Practice 2008

Singleton, Susan • £145 ISBN: 978-185418632-4

- Do you want to know how to use the Act to obtain information about your own competitors?
- Are you worried about making your contracts fully confidential?

These and many other issues are expertly dealt with in this valuable new report.

This report shows how businesses can ensure that they don't disclose information inadvertently and how to protect their own information by drafting new contracts in the right way. Susan Singleton has advised many clients in all sectors on the FOIA from a practical standpoint.

International Commercial Agreements

Attree, Rebecca • £99 ISBN: 978-185418286-9

This report appears at an exciting time for international commercial lawyers: new legislation, fresh opportunities – and the challenge of understanding fully how to exploit them.

Recent changes to EC Competition Law have made a significant impact upon parties' freedom to contract commercially, generally giving them greater flexibility. In the field of e-commerce, the EC has issued a welter of laws that are in the course of being implemented into national laws.

The report explains the principles and techniques of successful international negotiation and provides a valuable insight into the commercial points to be considered as a result of the laws relating to:

- pre-contract
- private international law
- resolving disputes (including alternative methods, such as mediation)
- competition law
- drafting common clauses
- and contracting electronically

Software Contract Agreements

Bond, Robert • £145 ISBN: 978-185418692-8

A thorough explanation of the law combined with expert guidance on negotiating and drafting the best contract for your client.

- A clear explanation of the law relating to computer contracts with particular emphasis on software licenses
- A wealth of advice, tips and techniques for successful contract negotiation and drafting
- Leading author: an expert with over 25 years' experience in IP/IT law in a wide range of sectors
- Valuable sample contracts

Achieving Business Excellence, Quality and Performance Improvement

Chapman, Colin & Hopper, Dennis • £99 ISBN: 978-185418018-6

This valuable briefing identifies all the areas critical to developing an effective performance improvement process. It is a practical guide to the use of business excellence models and frameworks, quality standards, benchmarking tools, self-assessment programmes and the latest performance improvement initiatives.

The Commercial Exploitation of Intellectual Property Rights by Licensing

DesForges, Charles • £99 ISBN: 978-185418285-4

This report will show you – whether as licensor or licensee – how to identify and secure profitable opportunities, strategies and techniques for negotiating the best agreement, and finally the techniques of successfully managing a license operation.

Intellectual Property Protection and Enforcement

Brazell, Lorna • £99 ISBN: 978-185418054-4

Incorporating the latest developments in IP law, this briefing reviews each of the principal forms of intellectual property right available in the United Kingdom, describing the nature of the right itself and explaining: How rights arise or can be obtained, How rights can be exploited, What is necessary to protect rights from erosion or loss, What actions will constitute infringement of a right, under either civil (enforced by the owner) or criminal (enforced by public authorities) law, What remedies are available to the owner of the right, once infringement has been proved.

Each chapter can be read on its own for convenient reference, and the introduction to each chapter also makes it clear where awareness of another section may be useful.

Waste Management: The changing legislative climate

Hand, Caroline • £69 ISBN: 978-185418367-5

This valuable briefing explains what all the new legislation, directives and regulations mean in practice and what you need to do to stay within the law. Recent far-reaching changes to the law and practice affect everyone – commerce and industry, central and local government and householders.

Websites and the Law

Singleton, Susan • £99 ISBN: 978-185418331-6

Is your company/client website legal? Do you know what information you are required by law to put on it? What can you do with people's personal data sent to your website? This briefing deals with all the practical legal issues which arise with websites – both those sites which sell goods or services and those which advertise.

A Practical Guide to Knowledge Management

Brelade, Sue & Harman, Chris • £99 ISBN: 978-185418230-2

An expert but jargon-free guide to enable you to manage the knowledge in your organisation successfully and to identify, gather and use that knowledge to maximum advantage.

Analyse your Business – A performance health check

O'Connor, Carol • £99 ISBN: 978-185418170-1

This briefing offers the tools and techniques for company-wide analysis and is essential reading for business leaders responsible for corporate performance. Its purpose is to put minor issues into perspective and discourage the use of quick fix solutions for bigger problems.

Tendering & Negotiating MoD Contracts

Boyce, Tim • £99 ISBN: 978-185418276-0

This specially commissioned report aims to draw out the main principles, processes and procedures involved in tendering and negotiating MoD contracts. As Tim Boyce writes in the Introduction, 'it is important to realise that the SPI embraces a conceptual shift in the role of the MoD procurers'.

What does this 'huge shift in thinking' mean for contractors? How exactly has the role of MoD purchasing changed? This briefing covers every aspect of competitive tendering, negotiation and contractual negotiations in this new era. There can be few people who combine Tim Boyce's experience and expertise with a gift for explaining issues and procedures with such clarity.

Understanding SMART Procurement in the MOD

Boyce, Tim • £99 ISBN: 978-185418164-0

The main thrust of this report is on issues to do with strategy, organisation and processes. The single most encouraging and exciting feature of the SMART procurement initiative is that it embraces the need to change the culture. There is a commitment within the high political echelon of the MoD to make this change happen. Probably the greatest single challenge is to ensure that this commitment is maintained through the inevitable changes of personality at the political and senior management level.

IT Governance

Norfolk, David • £99 ISBN: 978-185418371-2

This specially commissioned briefing sets out what the latest legislation says and what it means, its impact on the organisation as a whole and on the IT group specifically, and how to implement an effective IT governance initiative in your company.

For full details of any title, and to view sample extracts, please visit:
www.thorogoodpublishing.co.uk

Practical Techniques for Effective Project Investment Appraisal

Tiffin, Ralph • £99 ISBN: 978-185418099-5

How to ensure you have a reliable system in place. Spending money on projects automatically necessitates an effective appraisal system – a way of deciding whether the correct decisions on investment have been made.

Project Risk Management: The commercial dimension

Boyce, Tim • £95 ISBN: 978-185418257-9

This briefing will show you how to fully appreciate all the commercial dimensions of important projects and understand how to identify all the risks during the pre-contract bidding phase.

Strategy Implementation Through Project Management

Grundy, Tony • £99 ISBN: 978-185418250-0

The gap: Far too few managers know how to apply project management techniques to their strategic planning. The result is often strategy that is poorly thought out and executed.

The answer: Strategic project management is a new and powerful process designed to manage complex projects by combining traditional business analysis with project management techniques.

Surviving a Corporate Crisis: 100 things you need to know

Batchelor, Paul • £99 ISBN: 978-185418208-1

Seven out of ten organisations that experience a corporate crisis go out of business within 18 months. This briefing not only covers remedial action after the event but offers expert advice on preparing every department and every key player of the organisation so that, should a crisis occur, damage of every kind is limited as far as possible.

Technical Aspects of Business Leases: Overcoming the practical difficulties

Dowden, Malcolm • £99 ISBN: 978-185418194-7

The purpose of this briefing is to highlight areas where technical issues might lead to practical difficulties, and to give clear guidance to help those involved in property management avoid the pitfalls.

FINANCE

Tax Planning for Businesses and their Owners

Hughes, Peter • £145 ISBN: 978-185418402-3

Written for business owners and managers, this special report offers expert advice on the tax implications of your business decisions – guiding you in making the right business and personal choices for tax reduction.

Trade Secrets of Business Disposals

Pearson, Barrie • £145 ISBN: 978-185418321-7

If you're like most people, you'll only get one chance to sell your business and to capitalise on years of hard work and planning. You can either fluff it, or make sure you get the best possible advisor and become financially secure for life, and possibly very rich. This briefing shows you how to make your business 'investor-ready' for maximum capital return.

Trade Secrets of Business Acquisitions

Pearson, Barrie • £145 ISBN: 978-185418366-8

In this invaluable new briefing one of the City's most successful deal-makers distils 40 years' experience as both principal and advisor. "Losing a deal by adopting the wrong tactics is unforgiveable" he writes, but it happens all too often. This briefing offers both professional advisors and principals the opportunity to transform their rate of success, clarifying hard truths and highlighting avoidable mistakes. It is laced throughout with proven tactical advice to ensure that both deals and post-acquisition management are carried out with maximum success.

VAT Liability and the Implications of Commercial Property Transactions

Buss, Tim • £145 ISBN: 978-185418307-1

The option to tax is a major VAT planning tool but you have got to get the detail right to take full advantage – and getting it wrong can be very costly. This briefing shows you how to plan for maximum advantage and avoid costly mistakes.

EMPLOYMENT LAW

Data Protection Law for Employers 2008

Singleton, Susan • £145 ISBN: 978-185418626-3

This briefing seeks to summarise the application of the Act to the employment discipline. It concentrates on the areas, which are useful and practical to employers by examining the Information Commissioner's Office code of practice. It answers many of the mundane, day-to-day data protections issues that employers and those who are responsible for personal data need to know.

Discrimination Law and Employment Issues

Martin, David • £145 ISBN: 978-185418678-2

The Age Discrimination Act is billed by lawyers as the most significant change in employment law since the 1970s. In addition to sex and race discrimination laws, in the last two years employers have also had to cope with sexual orientation discrimination and religious discrimination. David Martin, an expert on employment law and practice, analyses the practical aspects of dealing with each of the anti-discrimination laws. He demonstrates how to ensure that paperwork and systems comply totally with the law, and he provides a range of helpful case studies to illustrate the key issues and bring them to life.

Effective Recruitment: A practical guide to staying within the law

Leighton, Patricia & Proctor, Giles • £145 ISBN: 978-185418683-6

The ways to undertake the task continue to grow, making the decision as to how best to recruit for a given employment situation more complex. This specialist text is responding to a number of imperatives, including legal ones. There have been, and are, anticipated changes that make it essential that recruitment practitioners act both effectively and within the law.

Employee Sickness and Fitness for Work: Successfully dealing with the legal system

Howard, Gillian • £99 ISBN: 978-185418281-4

Many executives see employment law as an obstacle course or, even worse, an opponent – but it can contribute positively to keeping employees fit and productive. This briefing will show you how to get the best out of your employees, from recruitment to retirement, while protecting yourself and your firm to the full.

Employment Law Aspects of Mergers and Acquisitions: A practical guide

Ryley, Michael • £99 ISBN: 978-185418363-7

This report will help you to understand the key practical and legal issues, achieve consensus and involvement at all levels, understand and implement TUPE regulations and identify the documentation that needs to be drafted or reviewed within the context of a merger, acquisition or disposal.

Navigating Health and Safety Law: Ensuring compliance and minimising risk

Pope, Chris • £99 ISBN: 978-185418353-8

If you have already been challenged by the insurer, inspector, or one of your workforce about the status of your health and safety this briefing will give you a workable answer to questions like Is my health and safety policy legally compliant? How do I avoid being liable for an employees ill health arising from previous employment? Who should carry out safety inspections – is it my responsibility?

Successfully Defending Employment Tribunal Cases

Hunt, Dennis • £99 ISBN: 978-185418267-8

Sweeping changes to the way employment tribunal claims are dealt with have increased the risk of higher costs and more expensive claims. This indispensable report covers all the changes and their implications for HR professionals.

The Thorogood Promise

If you are not totally satisfied and you return a publication in mint condition within 14 days of receipt, we will refund the cost of the publication, no questions asked.

Applying the Employment Act 2002: Crucial developments for employers and employees

Williams, Audrey • £99 ISBN: 978-185418253-1

The Act represents a major shift in the commercial environment, with far-reaching changes for employers and employees. The consequences of getting it wrong, for both employer and employee, will be considerable – financial and otherwise. The Act affects nearly every aspect of the workplace.

Dismissal and Grievance Procedures

Hunt, Dennis • £99 ISBN: 978-185418376-7

This briefing explains what all the regulations say and what steps you need to take to operate effective dismissal, disciplinary and grievance procedures. It covers all the requirements of the Disputes Resolution Procedures that came into effect in October 2004. It tells you where and when the regulations apply – and what you need to do.

Enabling Beyond Empowerment

Williams, Michael • £99 ISBN: 978-185418084-1

By applying the range of practical management techniques detailed in this briefing, you can provide the authority and means to empower in a way that substantially reduces the dangers.

Flexible Working

Williams, Audrey • £99 ISBN: 978-185418306-4

Recent research shows that far too many individuals, as well as firms, are unaware of flexible working rights. How employers and employees deal with them is of crucial – and increasing – importance to both. This briefing clarifies the law, sets out the rights of employer and employee, and offers valuable practical advice on best practice.

How to Turn your HR Strategy into Reality

Grundy, Tony • £99 ISBN: 978-185418183-1

From a diagnosis of HR issues to an analysis of the external and internal future environment of your company and the effect on your human resources – this is practical information aimed at HR and senior line managers.

Internal Communications

Farrant, James • £99 ISBN: 978-185418149-7

There is growing evidence that the organisations that 'get it right' reap dividends in corporate energy and enhanced performance. In these organisations, internal communications have equal status with the external communications functions. This practical briefing will show you how internal communications, taken in their widest sense, can improve the performance of organisations.

Mergers and Acquisitions: Confronting the organisation and people issues

Thomas, Mark • £145 ISBN: 978-185418676-8

Why do so many mergers and acquisitions end in tears and reduced shareholder value? This report will help you to understand the key practical and legal issues, achieve consensus and involvement at all levels, understand and implement TUPE regulations and identify the documentation that needs to be drafted or reviewed.

New Ways of Working

Jupp, Stephen • £99 ISBN: 978-185418169-5

New ways of working examines the nature of the work done in an organisation and seeks to optimise the working practices and the whole context in which the work takes place. It is more about promoting the best ways of doing things than simple cost driven change. Although it emphasises the importance of business and organisation, it spans the concerns of people, property, technology, community and environment.

Power Over Stress at Work

Araoz, Daniel • £99 ISBN: 978-185418176-3

The HR manager can learn how to deal creatively with stress from the information in this briefing and pass on their knowledge down the ranks. He or she will then halt the downward spiral of diffusing stress and produce a more positive knock-on effect – namely to increase the productivity of the entire workforce and reduce absenteeism resulting from this terrible illness.

Reviewing and Changing Contracts of Employment

Phillips, Annelise; Player, Thomas & Rome, Paula • £99 ISBN: 978-185418296-8

The Employment Act 2002 has raised the stakes. Imperfect understanding of the law and poor drafting will now be very costly. This briefing will:

- Ensure that you have a total grip on what should be in a contract and what should not
- Explain step by step how to achieve changes in the contract of employment without causing problems
- Enable you to protect clients' sensitive business information
- Enhance your understanding of potential conflict areas and your ability to manage disputes effectively.

Trade Secrets of Using e-Learning in Training

Bray, Tony • £99 ISBN: 978-185418326-2

Definitely not for 'techies', this briefing is practical and jargon-free – giving you step-by-step skills and processes to enable you to design effective e-learning products with confidence.

Transforming HR

Hunter, Ian and Saunders, Jane • £99 ISBN: 978-185418361-3

The blue-print for the future of HR – how to deliver proven value to your Board, business and colleagues. The briefing is based on interviews with 60 HR leaders from across industry and public and not for profit sectors. The briefing covers HR outsourcing and shared services.

MARKETING, PR AND SALES

Corporate Community Investment

Genasi, Chris • £99 ISBN: 978-185418192-3

Supporting good causes is big business – and good business. Corporate community investment (CCI) is the general term for companies' support of good causes, and is a very fast growing area of PR and marketing.

Defending your Reputation

Taylor, Simon • £99 ISBN: 978-185418251-7

'Buildings can be rebuilt, IT systems replaced, people can be recruited, but a reputation lost can never be regained…The media will publish a story – you may as well ensure it is your story' *Simon Taylor.* 'News is whatever someone, somewhere, does not want published' *William Randolph Hearst* When a major crisis does suddenly break, how ready will you be to defend your reputation?

Implementing an Integrated Marketing Communications Strategy

Hart, Norman • £99 ISBN: 978-185418120-6

Get ahead and stay ahead of your competition through better integration of your marketing communications. Norman Hart was an international consultant, lecturer and author on marketing, advertising and public relations. His books included *The CIM Marketing Dictionary, Strategic Public Relations, The Practice of Advertising* and *Industrial Marketing Communications.*

Insights into Understanding the Financial Media: An insider's view

Scott, Simon • £99 ISBN: 978-185418083-4

This practical report will help you understand the way the financial print and broadcast media works in the UK. It will also provide you with techniques and guidelines on how to communicate with the financial media in the most effective way, to help you achieve accurate and positive coverage of your organisation and its operations.

Lobbying and the Media: Working with politicians and journalists

Burrell, Michael • £99 ISBN: 978-185418240-1

Lobbying is an art form rather than a science, so there is inevitably an element of judgement in what line to take. The best lobbying is always based on accurate, up-to-date information and on a well-argued case, founded on credible evidence, and delivered to the right audiences in the right tone of voice at the right time. Sounds simple, but it isn't. This expert briefing explains the knowledge and techniques required.

Managing Corporate Reputation: The new currency

Dalton, John & Croft, Susan • £99 ISBN: 978-185418272-2

ENRON, WORLDCOM... who next? At a time when trust in corporations has plummeted to new depths, knowing how to manage corporate reputation professionally and effectively has never been more crucial. This briefing shows you how to:

- Develop PR, brands and relationship management as the vanguards of your corporate reputation
- Strengthen your internal as well as external communications
- Improve the effective management of your stakeholders

Practical Techniques for Effective Lobbying

Miller, Charles • £99 ISBN: 978-185418089-6

Understanding the system and the process in which it works is essential to lobbying effectively. Uncoordinated, uncontrolled and badly planned approaches will do more harm than good, and risk antagonising the people you most want to influence. This briefing provides the techniques required for effective lobbying.

Public Affairs Techniques for Business

Wynne-Davies, Peter • £99 ISBN: 978-185418175-6

This briefing shows in practical terms how you can counter potential threats through a professionally structured and implemented public affairs campaign. Today's successful companies recognise that in order to survive and prosper a comprehensive and disciplined approach to public affairs is no longer just a useful asset, it is now a necessity.

Selling Skills for Professionals

Tasso, Kim • £99 ISBN: 978-185418179-4

Many professionals still feel awkward about really selling their professional services. They are not usually trained in selling. This is a much-needed briefing which addresses the unique concerns of professionals who wish to sell their services successfully and to feel comfortable doing so.

Strategic Customer Planning

Melkman, Alan • £95 ISBN: 978-185418388-0

This is very much a 'how to' briefing. After reading those parts that are relevant to your business, you will be able to compile a powerful customer plan that will work within your particular organisation for you. Charts, checklists and diagrams throughout.

Strategic Planning in Public Relations

Knights, Kieran • £145 ISBN: 978-185418225-8

Tips and techniques to aid you in a new approach to campaign planning. Strategic planning is a fresh approach to PR. An approach that is *fact-based* and scientific, clearly presenting the arguments for a campaign proposal backed with *evidence*. This briefing provides valuable tips and techniques to improve your PR and campaign planning.

Successful Competitive Tendering

Woodhams, Jeff • £99 ISBN: 978-185418235-7

To win business, you must make a convincing case. This briefing will help you become more skillful, and more successful in your tendering.

Techniques for Ensuring PR Coverage in the Regional Media: An insider's view

Imeson, Mike • £99 ISBN: 978-185418019-3

This in-depth briefing will give you the tools and techniques you need to enjoy the opportunities offered by the regional and local media. It offers you practical guidance and advice on how to apply them with maximum effect for your next PR campaign.

Order Form

FIVE WAYS TO ORDER

1 Tel: +44 (0)1235 465 500

2 Fax: +44 (0)1235 465 556

3 Email: direct.orders@marston.co.uk

4 Web: www.thorogoodpublishing.co.uk

5 Post: Marston Book Services, 10-12 Rivington Street, London EC2A 3DU

Title	ISBN	Price	Authors	Qty
Commercial Contracts: Legal principles and drafting	978-185418702-4	£145	Burnett, Rachel	
Commercial Litigation: Damages and other remedies for breach of contract	978-185418397-2	£145	Ribeiro, Robert	
Corporate Governance	978-185418354-5	£99	Martin, David	
Email: Legal issues	978-185418256-0	£145	Singleton, Susan	
Freedom of Information Act	978-185418347-7	£145	Singleton, Susan	
International Commercial Agreements	978-185418286-9	£99	Attree, Rebecca	
Insights into Successfully Managing the In-house Legal Function	978-185418174-9	£95	O'Meara, Barry	
Software Contract Agreements	978-185418692-8	£145	Bond, Robert	
Achieving Business Excellence, Quality and Performance Improvement	978-185418018-6	£99	Chapman, Colin & Hopper, Dennis	
The Commercial Exploitation of Intellectual Property Rights by Licensing	978-185418285-4	£99	DesForges, Charles	
Intellectual Property Protection and Enforcement	978-185418054-4	£99	Brazell, Lorna	
Waste Management: The changing legislative climate	978-185418367-5	£69	Hand, Caroline	
Websites and the Law	978-185418331-6	£99	Singleton, Susan	
A Practical Guide to Knowledge Management	978-185418230-2	£99	Brelade, Sue & Harman, Chris	
Analyse your Business – A performance health check	978-185418170-1	£99	O'Connor, Carol	
Tendering & Negotiating MoD Contracts	978-185418276-0	£99	Boyce, Tim	
Understanding SMART Procurement in the MOD	978-185418164-0	£99	Boyce, Tim	

Title	ISBN	Price	Authors	Qty
IT Governance	978-185418371-2	£99	Norfolk, David	
Practical Techniques for Effective Project Investment Appraisal	978-185418099-5	£99	Tiffin, Ralph	
Project Risk Management: The commercial dimension	978-185418257-9	£99	Boyce, Tim	
Strategy Implementation Through Project Management	978-185418250-0	£99	Grundy, Tony	
Surviving a Corporate Crisis: 100 things you need to know	978-185418208-1	£90	Batchelor, Paul	
Technical Aspects of Business Leases: Overcoming the practical difficulties	978-185418194-7	£99	Dowden, Malcolm	
Tax Planning for Businesses and their Owners	978-185418334-7	£145	Hughes, Peter	
Trade Secrets of Business Disposals	978-185418321-7	£145	Pearson, Barrie	
Trade Secrets of Business Acquisitions	978-185418366-8	£145	Pearson, Barrie	
VAT Liability and the Implications of Commercial Property Transactions	978-185418307-1	£145	Buss, Tim	
Data Protection Law for Employers	978-185418283-8	£145	Singleton, Susan	
Discrimination Law and Employment Issues	978-185418339-2	£145	Martin, David	
Effective Recruitment: A practical guide to staying within the law	978-185418683-6	£145	Leighton, Patricia & Proctor, Giles	
Employee Sickness and Fitness for Work: Successfully dealing with the legal system	978-185418281-4	£99	Howard, Gillian	
Employment Law Aspects of Mergers and Acquisitions: A practical guide	978-185418363-7	£99	Ryley, Michael	
Navigating Health and Safety Law: Ensuring compliance and minimising risk	978-185418353-8	£99	Pope, Chris	
Successfully Defending Employment Tribunal Cases	978-185418267-8	£99	Hunt, Dennis	
Applying the Employment Act 2002: Crucial developments for employers and employees	978-185418253-1	£99	Williams, Audrey	
Dismissal and Grievance Procedures	978-185418376-7	£99	Hunt, Dennis	
Enabling Beyond Empowerment	978-185418084-1	£99	Williams, Michael	
Flexible Working	978-185418306-4	£99	Williams, Audrey	
How to Turn your HR Strategy into Reality	978-185418183-1	£99	Grundy, Tony	
Internal Communications	978-185418149-7	£99	Farrant, James	
Mergers and Acquisitions: Confronting the organisation and people issues	978-185418676-8	£145	Thomas, Mark	
New Ways of Working	978-185418169-5	£99	Jupp, Stephen	
Power Over Stress at Work	978-185418176-3	£99	Araoz, Daniel	
Reviewing and Changing Contracts of Employment	978-185418296-8	£99	Phillips, Annelise; Player, Thomas & Rome, Paula	
Trade Secrets of Using e-Learning in Training	978-185418326-2	£99	Bray, Tony	
Transforming HR	978-185418361-3	£99	Hunter, Ian and Saunders, Jane	
Corporate Community Investment	978-185418192-3	£99	Genasi, Chris	
Defending your Reputation	978-185418251-7	£99	Taylor, Simon	
Implementing an Integrated Marketing Communications Strategy	978-185418120-6	£99	Hart, Norman	

Title	ISBN	Price	Authors	Qty
Insights into Understanding the Financial Media: An insider's view	978-185418083-4	£99	Scott, Simon	
Lobbying and the Media: Working with politicians and journalists	978-185418240-1	£99	Burrell, Michael	
Managing Corporate Reputation: The new currency	978-185418272-2	£99	Dalton, John & Croft, Susan	
Practical Techniques for Effective Lobbying	978-185418089-6	£99	Miller, Charles	
Public Affairs Techniques for Business	978-185418175-6	£99	Wynne-Davies, Peter	
Selling Skills for Professionals	978-185418179-4	£99	Tasso, Kim	
Strategic Customer Planning	978-185418388-0	£99	Melkman, Alan	
Strategic Planning in Public Relations	978-185418225-8	£145	Knights, Kieran	
Successful Competitive Tendering	978-185418235-7	£99	Woodhams, Jeff	
Techniques for Ensuring PR Coverage in the Regional Media: An insider's view	978-185418019-3	£99	Imeson, Mike	

YOUR DETAILS

Please note that payment is required before briefings are dispatched. If paying by credit card, the address given below must be that of the cardholder.

Please use BLOCK capitals.

Name ____________________

Position ____________________

Company ____________________

Address ____________________

____

____________________ Postcode ____________

Country ____________________

Tel ____________________

Fax ____________________

Email ____________________

PAYMENT DETAILS

☐ I enclose a cheque for £ __________ made payable to MARSTON BOOK SERVICES

☐ Please invoice me

☐ Please charge my credit card

☐ Mastercard ☐ Visa ☐ Barclaycard ☐ American Express ☐ Switch ☐ Connect

Card no. ____________________ Expiry date ____________________

Valid from ____________________ Issue number ____________________

Cardholder's signature ____________________

☐ I have paid by bank transfer [BACS]: Barclays Bank, sort code 20-65-18, account ____________

POSTAGE AND PACKAGING

UK: Postage and packaging is FREE • **OVERSEAS**: £10 for the first copy and £5 for each additional copy

Please quote reference: "**Briefing**" when purchasing